Jean Laplace

AN EXPERIENCE OF LIFE IN THE SPIRIT

Ten Days
in the Tradition
of the Spiritual Exercises

translated by
JOHN R. MOONEY, S.J.

Franciscan Herald Press
1434 West 51st Street, Chicago 60609

Originally published as *Une Expérience de la Vie dans l'Esprit*. © Chalet, Lyon, France 1973.

American edition. Franciscan Publications. 1977.

Translation © T. Shand Publications London NW11.

ISBN America 0-8-0594-1.

Imprimatur, Lyon, le 30 December 72, P. Bony, c.d.

AN EXPERIENCE OF LIFE
IN THE SPIRIT

An Experience of Life in the Spirit:
Ten Days in the Tradition of the Spiritual
Exercises.

Jean Laplace, S.J.

Translated by John R. Mooney, S.J.

Table of Contents

7

9

Translator's Note

Father Jean Laplace is already known to many English-speaking readers for his works on spiritual direction. In *An Experience of Life in the Spirit* he has attempted to provide a tool for both retreatants and retreat directors. For the retreatant, he charts out an itinerary through the *Spiritual Exercises* of St. Ignatius; for the retreat director, he indicates how to accompany the retreatant on this journey. In doing so, he has tried to avoid a literarily pleasing discussion on the *theory* of the *Exercises* and tried instead to draw up a practical manual on how to guarantee the human component in the *experience* of the *Exercises*.

As usual, references to the *Spiritual Exercises* (e.g., *Ex.* 15) indicate the standard numeration according to sections, not the pagination of a particular edition.

On a personal note, I would like to thank Frank Hulefield, s.j., Yvette Sentner, and Ellen Nolan, who generously helped in the various stages of this translation, and Tom Burke, s.j., director of the Program to Adapt the *Spiritual Exercises*, who encouraged the project from the beginning.

Itinerary and Accompaniment

It is not easy to find a title that accurately describes the purpose of a book. In spiritual matters, words tend to be ambiguous. Someone suggested the title "the understanding of the heart"; but this would have required a long explanation. Moreover, as pretentious as this may sound, this book is not like other books. It is not meant to be read but to be used. It is an itinerary for an experience and, at the same time, an accompaniment. If anyone satisfies himself with merely leafing through these pages without testing their contents in his life, he would be in no position to assess this book. That is why, despite the possible ambiguities, I have kept the word "experience".

Not just any experience, but an experience of the life of the Spirit. This experience presupposes that the person undertaking it believes in the action of the Holy Spirit, who makes Jesus Christ take shape in us and makes us live a life of love. And there is a second difficulty: hasn't the Holy Spirit remained the unknown God for many people? And don't matters of the spiritual life seem unreal to many people . . ., at least the spiritual life as presented by tradition, and by us following that tradition?

As a matter of fact, these pages are the result of twenty years of experience: from four-day retreats to thirty-day retreats, with all the various kinds in between. Ten years ago I published, in loose-leaf form, an outline used in ten-day retreats. These notes have been out of print for some time. Various people have asked me to republish them in a finished form. Yet how can you fix upon paper a life that continues to develop – the lives of the retreatants and the director's life along with theirs.

I am allowing these pages to be printed with the hope that no one mistakes their nature or their usage. They are like residues of experience. The most fitting form for them is that of the maxims of the Fathers of the desert, like highly compact thoughts which show no logical development but rather invite us to enter into an ever-present reality. The ideal is that the reader, having read this book – or simply several pages – would close the book, forget it, and let prayer rise up within his heart.

In its entirety, this can constitute what we ordinarily call a retreat, as long as it does not freeze the plan of the retreat into rigidity. For a retreat plan serves its purpose only if adapted to each individual person or group. I present a ten-day retreat because that is the form in which I usually gave the *Exercises*. But anyone who uses these notes, especially if he is alone, should be able to shorten or lengthen his retreat as he wishes. Another question: is it necessary, in following this itinerary, to retire into a house of prayer? From time to time this is good. But it is not always possible. Why not follow this itinerary at home, devoting some time to it each day and spreading out the entire thing over several weeks or months? Anything is possible.

That last remark evokes another. What I am presenting here is not just an aid for making a retreat; it is a formation in the life of the Spirit. Undoubtedly it is good to isolate oneself from time to time to make these ten days, but the reality that is communicated to us on such occasions cannot be exhausted once and for all. The seed takes years to produce its fruit and must be preserved in the humdrum of daily life. Its development in real life makes visible what was hidden and verifies its authenticity. And, just as this experience is meant to transform the whole of life, so also it can exclude no category of persons; for those who give themselves to this experience are searching for God in the very depths of their being. The spiritual life is not the private domain of any person or social class. We used to distinguish between retreats for laymen, for priests, for religious, for youth, etc. In certain ways this specialization has its advantages; in other ways it is regrettable. This was frequently my experience during retreats that grouped together laymen, married people, priests, single people, and religious. Such mixed groups help a person discover his essential core, which is beneath and beyond such specific differences. As I shall point out later, the conditions required for admitting a person to such an experience are not to be found in his social class or his societal role or his education but rather in his human maturity and in a certain interior docility.

I claim to be in the tradition of the *Spiritual Exercises*. Of course, I mean those of St. Ignatius. Does that mean that these pages propose to be either an interpretation or an adaptation of those *Exercises*? Both are the business of the exegetes, the historians of spirituality, and the researchers. Their work, like the work of those who try to interpret the Word of God or to put it into a modern idiom, is necessary. It would be dangerous to ignore such work. It would also be dangerous to limit oneself to the letter of the *Exercises*, ignoring the great tradition of the Church, both before and after the *Exercises*, in the West as well as in the East; for our failure to appreciate this tradition of spirituality does us great harm. However, life does not wait for our research. We shall all be dead before the researchers have finished their work. My point of view is that of the educator, for whom life awakens life. It is the viewpoint of a man who believes in the Holy Spirit and has helped himself, in his own way, with the means that tradition and his own experience have taught him: he now shares what he lives by, so that others – through their contact with him – may experience an awakening to the life of the Spirit who dwells in us.

This pedagogical point of view explains the book's order of presentation. Here I have kept the division into days, so that the book can be used more easily in the course of a retreat. Roughly speaking, the notes for each day consist of a general orientation, some counsels on prayer, some texts to help one's prayer, and finally some directives on discernment. Of themselves, these elements do not follow from one to another; their unity is achieved in the experience itself. That is why it is not good to read all the notes at one sitting, but rather as experience makes them necessary.

There is an itinerary. It is that of the *Exercises*, since they make a person pass through the major stages of the Christian experience and help him discern, by following these *Exercises*, what God wants of him. But the presentation of this itinerary is not done through some abstract instruction, although such instruction is necessary, especially in the beginning. Still, my method of presentation intends not to construct some spiritual synthesis but to personalize the life of faith in an atmosphere of growing freedom. The object of our faith should become the source of unity and of life.

Why not publish right away the notes I have used in giving

the thirty-day retreat? I believe that would be premature, despite the experiences I have already had with thirty-day retreats. Besides, this book can be used, if necessary, for such a retreat. A person need only proceed through it more slowly and give even more time to contemplating the mysteries of the life, death, and resurrection of Jesus.

All of this is nothing but a collection of exercises, samples, suggestions, invitations to travel – many different ways of preparing ourselves for the action of the Spirit in order to "seek and find the will of God in the disposition of our life" (*Exercises* §1).

Maison Saint-Joseph, La Bernerie
June 24, 1972, on the feast of St. John the Baptist

Before Entering into the Experience

It would be good to read these bits of advice in the course of the first day. They condense and draw together several annotations of the *Exercises*. It might also be useful to return to them during the retreat. They constitute a pedagogy of prayer that is valid for the whole of life.

However, it is important to take them for what they are: a means for preparing one's heart. Prayer is the work of the Holy Spirit. It is not primarily a matter of will, reflection, or sentiment. Nor can it ever be the direct result of some sort of instruction. A person could no more teach another person how to pray than he could create the experience of love for another person. The mystery of encounter remains the secret of each individual: Go into your room. . . . This is the law of all love, of God and of others. Thus, love and do what you want.

We can, however, help prepare ourselves better. The *Exercises* ready us for something that does not come from us, but without which our life would not be life. Who can live without loving? What Christian can live without praying?

This advice on prayer contains the necessary conditions for any spiritual experience. Its aim is to form in us those dispositions that open the heart to every action of the Holy Spirit, in particular self-acceptance. This disposition, whose nature will become clear little by little, is far from being a passive resignation. Self-acceptance is one element of the indifference that St. Ignatius requires for praying, for making the *Exercises*, and for leading a human life in harmony with God. It is an acceptance that is both openness to the future and confidence in God, the acceptance of being "a testing ground for the Holy Spirit" (Teilhard).

1. *The Length of Time. The Hour of Day*

"We should always try to be certain of having spent a full hour in the exercise. In fact, it is better to lengthen this period than to shorten it" (*Ex.* 12). In this profound experience of prayer, nothing can replace time. I doubt that I could ever have known what prayer is, if I had not decided at one time to pay the price for it, that is, to persevere in it. Afterwards, prayer is no longer the same; it becomes part of our very body. It is the same with prayer as with any art: ease is proportionate to regular practice.

There are numerous witnesses who could testify that this is the essential point. All the rest – reading, plans for one's life, discussions, notes – is secondary. No one enters here unless he decides to spend time on it – or waste time, as certain people might think.

In accepting the length of time for prayer, we make a preliminary act of faith in the Holy Spirit's operation in our hearts: we believe that grace can transform poor creatures like ourselves.

Concretely, this acceptance means four hours of prayer a day (or even five if the retreatant, following a suggestion of the *Exercises*, wants to get up during the night to pray).

This requirement is unbearable unless we add: each person should take his own situation into account. This is where the schedule gets its flexibility. Ideally, the *Exercises* are given individually. Each individual should find his own rhythm, even if he is making the *Exercises* in a group.

Submission to the duration of prayer makes us pass from the intellectual level to the spiritual level, from an instruction that has been received to an experience that has been lived. Anyone who contents himself with hearing a conference and reflecting on it or discussing it afterwards is limiting himself to mere criticism or mere ideas. Without his suspecting it, his gain will be merely apparent or fleeting. He is forcing truth to come to him, rather than letting himself be drawn by the truth. If he takes time, however, he cannot remain at that point. He will be forced to move towards God and to give himself over to him.

Let us not be anxious to know everything in advance, as if to insure ourselves against the risks. What is true of freedom and love is also true of prayer. We understand its nature only if we practise it day after day.

2. *How to Begin. Peace of Mind*

"Before entering into the prayer, I should rest my mind for a while, either seated or walking; and . . . I will reflect on where I am going and why" (*Ex.* 239). The body relaxes, the mind concentrates, and the heart opens up – all at the same time. This is the "Take off your shoes" addressed to Moses (Exodus 3) and the "Close your door and lock it" of the Sermon on the Mount (Mt. 6:6).

Many people imagine that preparation for prayer consists in settling upon a subject and determining its main points, as though they were then going to present some sort of pre-planned disquisition. It is enough to focus our mind on one point or another, in order to avoid vagueness. "Where to begin" is a frequent expression in the Journal of St. Ignatius. Thus the mind is at peace. That is why I here propose texts of Scripture as points of departure for prayer.

In focusing the mind, the whole person concentrates and simplifies himself. For prayer to awaken, it is important for the mind not to divide its attention among many objects. It focuses on just one point, to be more open to the inspiration which the Holy Spirit will communicate to him, using this point as a medium.

There are some retreat masters who want to say everything; they encumber the mind, prevent personal assimilation, and tire people out even before the prayer begins. There are some retreatants who fall into the same error: they would like to hear about everything; they want to use the retreat as an opportunity to bone up on all the latest ideas or all the newest books. Both forget that, in the course of these *Spiritual Exercises*, it is better to let "the Creator and Lord personally communicate himself to the devout soul" (*Ex.* 15).

The body participates in this concentration by its readiness: "seated or walking", that is, in a calm and relaxed attitude. We must learn that our bodily position is not something indifferent to prayer, no more than peaceful breathing is. One does not have to be a devotee of yoga or Zen to experience the truth of this. Whenever we allow ourselves to be totally taken up into a task, the whole body participates in our attention. "I will begin the meditation, now kneeling, now prostrate, now lying face up, now seated, now standing – always trying to seek what I desire" (*Ex.* 76). And if a particular posture is right for me, why would I want to change it?

The mind and the body become peaceful; and true attention becomes possible, the kind that does not tire. Whenever we leave prayer tense and nervous, it is always good to ask ourselves if something is wrong. Perhaps there is reason to change something in our procedure. Tension is a sign that we are putting too much stock in our own efforts, and that we do not yet understand what it means to be relaxed enough to be even more present.

3. *Total Commitment*

Anyone who undertakes the *Exercises* is offering God "his entire will and freedom, that the divine Majesty may use him and all he has according to his most holy will" (*Ex.* 5). Each person enters into prayer with everything he is: "his whole heart, his whole soul, his whole mind, and all his strength" (Mk. 12:30), his "entire being, mind, soul, and body" (1 Thes. 5:23), disarmed, defenceless, with his real life.

Many insist today that their whole life is a prayer. What does living mean for such persons? What is this life which they claim to be making into a prayer? Does "coming to God with one's life" mean bringing my bitterness, deceptions, and critiques and judgments about others into my prayer? We could say that "praying with one's very life" means, first of all, offering the whole complex that we are, so that God can purify it; it is to "ask God our Lord that all my intentions, actions, and operations may be directed purely to the service and praise of his divine Majesty" (*Ex.* 46).

In order to pray with one's very life, therefore, it is not enough to remain at the level of events or emotional reactions. What I offer God is a person with all his capacities to exist and to love, as well as his desire to see the Spirit penetrate into his depths, so that he may be given a new way of seeing and a new heart: "God, create for me a pure heart" (Ps. 51[50]:12). This means: when you pray, make an act of real freedom; go into your room, where you are your real self, without worrying about the opinions of others or about the correct formulas; and the Father who sees in secret will give you the gift of his Spirit.

Generosity, one of the most ambiguous words in the language of spirituality, does not consist in stirring up strong sentiments within oneself nor even in the service of the most noble causes. Rather it consists in descending a bit more deeply into what we really are and, through a willingness to look ourselves in the face, in presenting ourselves to the Lord so that he might accomplish his work in us. Freedom offers itself to grace. It is in this sense that prayer is never separated from the life and character of the individual.

Unfortunately, there are some for whom this language is still very strange. They run away from themselves, live in anxiety about how others see or judge them, and have not yet learned to know and accept themselves. It is to the extent that a person develops each day his human capacities, especially in the matter of human relationships and love, that he offers grace a foothold. Frequently we falsely set the two in opposition. Real presence to self is also presence to the reality of God, of others, of life. Everything is a whole.

4. *Spiritual Affectivity*

"The soul is not satisfied and filled by knowing a lot of facts but by feeling and tasting things in the depths of the heart" (*Ex.* 2). Certainly, when I enter into prayer, it is with a particular purpose: a certain "account to contemplate or meditate on" (*Ex.* 2), a certain project to consider, a certain word of a prayer whose meaning I want to contemplate (*Ex.* 249). As we have said, it is important to know where to begin and then to focus our attention.

But what then?

Of course, it is first of all the eye of the intelligence that tries to open itself to the truth, but not as though upon an object of study or of some intellectual consideration. What happens, rather, is like an artist's way of looking at a work: he draws near, he stands back, he lets it imprint itself within him, he savours it. This is what a person tries to do when he prays. He receives the Word. Under the influence of the unction which makes him recall things again (Jn. 14) and which "teaches him about all things" (1 Jn. 2), he ponders, he quietly repeats to himself what he has heard. That is why St. Ignatius counsels him "to rest at the point where he finds what he wants, without being anxious to go any further, until he finds himself satisfied" (*Ex.* 76).

"Tasting", "savouring", "resting": different words in an affective vocabulary, all of which say the same thing. Religious truth is not penetrated in the same way we penetrate objects of science, moving from one position to another in logical order. A single point, having been tasted, opens the way to others, just as in the *Credo*, where all the articles form a whole and where an understanding of one of the articles leads to an understanding of the others. We do not come to know God as an object in the world; we come to know him as a living person. His reality is bestowed upon us little by little, through the successive approaches of the heart. This procedure is not the denial of understanding, but the discovery of truth as life.

As we progressively enter into prayer, it is normal that we ask God for the spiritual gifts that make us know him, taste him, love him. The liturgy never ceases to ask God for relish, joy, delight – even for the sense of sin, which is just another way of experiencing God. St. Ignatius does the same. Both are in direct line with the prayer of Scripture and of the Psalms: "How sweet to my lips are your words." "My heart says to you: It is your face that I seek." "My heart and my flesh cry out to you with joy."

No one should be surprised at this kind of language. True, many could never imagine being thrilled by prayer. They approach it as a duty. Yet it would be a very strange pair of lovers who met only out of duty. If one's prayer is marked by dryness, this presents a problem whose causes should be investigated.

"The activity of the will, when we converse vocally or mentally with God our Lord, . . . demands a greater respect on our part" (*Ex.* 3). At the end of the exercise, one should "speak as a friend speaks with his friend" (*Ex.* 54).

At the outset of prayer, the mind was invited to rest itself, so that the heart could open itself to grace and taste God. At the end, the heart is invited to rest in the feeling of reality that God communicates to it. This is the prayer of the heart, the conversation with God where each person speaks as he hears, with the deepest kind of respect born of love.

Here it is no longer a question of rules, no more than in the case of those persons who have attained love. Love creates its own rules. The language of prayer is that of freedom, of love, of relationships. In the end, it is silence in adoration, wonder, and gratitude.

Many persons perhaps are put off by this call to affectivity. Still, a person becomes balanced only in loving. All the more so if we are giving ourselves to our creator! It is with our whole being that we must go to him. Thus, how can consecrated lives escape imbalance if they develop in dryness, fear, or ignorance of affectivity?

Here, as in ordinary life, we should not reject but rather educate our affectivity and purify it. This formation is one of the objectives of the discernment of spirits. How? By avoiding complacency and self-centredness. The satisfaction that accompanies self-giving and the encounter with another is willed by God; but if, upon experiencing it, I then seek to revivify it without some object's awakening it, I commit an impurity. Life and its difficulties will bring about the necessary purifications. My task consists in not dodging them, a task I must never refuse. I must come to the point where I want the other and God for themselves. Just like our growth in love, this task will never be finished.

Thus, the law of all affectivity, especially spiritual affectivity, is the object, the "thing": "to feel the things" (*Ex.* 2). True prayer, far from leading a person to turn in upon himself, is, like true love, a "getting outside oneself". If it turns inward, this is a clear sign that it is not a search for God but for oneself.

We soon detect counterfeit prayer through its resultant sadness, hardness of heart, contempt for others, and loss of the taste for life and for communication.

It should be rather obvious that the experience of true prayer, which is the experience of a relationship in the Spirit, is not a stranger to the experience we have of love in our relations with others. How can a person understand the language of love of God if he does not understand the language of love of others? We can speak only of those things we know. Many difficulties supposedly of a spiritual nature are rooted in a misunderstanding or lack of development on the human level.

Let us add that, the greater the human capacities of a person, the more necessary this affective balance on the spiritual level becomes. Without it, a serious gap develops between a human life that is evolving and a spiritual life that is drying up and becoming more infantile. Here we are touching upon one of the most frequent causes of crises in the religious life.

Helps for Achieving This Experience

"So that the director and the retreatant may find more help and profit . . .," writes St. Ignatius (*Ex.* 22) in speaking of the mutual confidence necessary for the progress of the *Exercises*. Whether the *Exercises* are made individually or in a group, the participants should consider themselves to be sharing a work of the Holy Spirit. Their being together should be a help for all, individually and collectively.

1. *The Conference*

Its purpose is not to give a doctrinal exposition, although there is a doctrine underlying this journey. Rather, through the instruction given, the conference tries to set an experience into motion and to show, in so far as possible, how to bring it to completion.

For all practical purposes, the conference can have two parts. The first consists of the counsels which make up the accompaniment. They are the common helps for prayer and discernment, designed to fit the various stages of the experience. They do not take the place of private conferences, but they do help make such conferences briefer and more precise. Secondly, there are orientations for prayer. For this purpose, several texts can be presented succinctly, more by way of suggestions than of explanations. If the explanation is too long, we become saturated; and then our tendency is to discuss or take notes rather than to pray.

In actual practice, one conference a day seems to be enough. The best time for it is in the morning. In this way, the mind, having got what it needs, is not interrupted thereafter in its own train of thought. It is none the less good, as the last thing in the evening, to take a few minutes to indicate the orientation of prayer for the next day.

We should say a word on how to listen. We should resemble the fourth kind of ground in the parable: a disencumbered, open, peaceful heart, as if the words we hear have just re-awakened a dormant truth we already possess. One should not be concerned about remembering everything or getting everything down in his notes, but rather about preparing his heart for prayer and for the day to come. Watch out how you take notes! The trees can sometimes hide the forest.

This procedure presupposes that all parties are convinced that the true master is the one who speaks not to the ears but to the heart. If we do not try to hear *him*, through the medium of man's words, "how many will leave without having heard a thing?" (Augustine) As a matter of fact, even if an exchange is not possible during the conference, this does not make it any less a sharing in the one truth of which we are all disciples. I who speak give you what I have. What will you do with it? I do not know. I open myself to you without defences, telling you what the Spirit inspires me to say in these circumstances. For your part, open yourself without reservations. No one can enter here with mere curiosity. Remain humble in your effort; do not fuss with the obscurities or impossibilities. The Lord will remove them in his good time, if you pray.

2. *Spiritual Dialogue*

The individual retreat remains the ideal. There the role of counselling is evident. The group retreat, nevertheless, has its usefulness: the instruction received, the formation of a Christian community. Each person should choose whichever he needs at a given time.

Individual help is equally necessary in the group retreat, especially at the beginning. The instructions, which to a certain extent take the place of individual direction, allow a person to proceed more quickly in his meetings with the director.

Should we establish a rule? The visits should be short and frequent, all the more frequent if we are unexperienced in this kind of retreat. For others who are more used to it, a mere chat during the course of the ten days might suffice. One thing is certain: if they take place at the right time, these visits can prevent many misunderstandings and mistakes, much discouragement and loss of time.

The purpose of these visits is the same as the purpose of the examen, which we shall discuss later. The main reason for these conferences is that they help us become aware of the way we are behaving, the lights received along the road, and the obstacles that alienate our freedom. In any case, each individual should decide what he wants to discuss with the director. The director, on the other hand, should tend to be reserved: his role is to accept what is confided to him and then to react to it. Unfortunately, many people could become uncomfortable with this silence; they want to be interrogated. We should recognize their uneasiness as a sign of some interior obstacle which ought to be clarified. Thus we shall be more free from it in the future.

It is good to formulate for ourselves and then to discuss our initial ideas about the experience under way. This could be the purpose of the first visit. Further experience might lead us to modify these ideas and to accept something other than what we first expected.

This manifestation of our thoughts is part of a whole tradition, whose boundaries extend beyond Christianity – that of the spiritual master. This tradition is based upon the law of all human education: alone, no one can form himself.

3. *Fraternal Sharing*

When a retreat is made in a group, it is good to offer those interested a chance to share their experiences during the course of the retreat. The point is neither to discuss nor to give or receive advice, but simply to share with a few other persons the lights we have received or the way in which we pray.

We can make several remarks about such a sharing.

All of those who participate in it should come freely. There is no such thing as merely auditing or observing: "I'll just check out how things go. If I like that kind of thing, I'll go back again." This sharing is a spiritual exercise, where, as in prayer, each individual involves his real self.

It is good if each group is limited to seven or eight members. If there are more, there is a danger that each person will not be able to speak in a relaxed manner. Or, again, some experienced speakers can take control, and the purpose of the sharing changes: it moves from a sharing of experiences to a discussion of ideas. Now, on the level of experience, everyone is equal.

In order to really hear what the other person is saying and to share oneself, it is not a bad idea to pause for a few moments of silence before going around the circle. A rich silence sets the tone for the sharing. If, in the course of this sharing, you feel a need to make some remark or to ask a question, this silence should be its source. Your purpose will not be to start an argument but to be able to hear better what the other is saying and to help him express himself better.

There should be no minutes or synthesis of such a sharing. What was said remains the secret of those who have shared these confidences. Our purpose here is not to judge anyone, whether ourselves or others, but rather to accept one another as each one follows the path that the Spirit marks out for him.

As far as possible, this experience should be continued over several days by the same participants. Perhaps, if the retreat is long enough, it would be better not to begin these meetings right away, but only on the third or fourth day. This gives the individual time to settle down into prayer. Let us also mention that, in the beginning, we can feel a certain clumsiness or difficulty in expressing ourselves. No use to force oneself. As in prayer, ease will come little by little. By the end, we shall be sharing ourselves as we are, without thinking about it; and this will add to the mutual joy, since each individual will have gained a new reassurance from the whole group.

This sharing does not replace the individual conference, but it often simplifies and facilitates it. It is possible that, in retreats with very precise objectives (like the choice of a state of life), such sharing should be discouraged. The experiences described by others might interfere with the direction we are following and even thwart it, especially if we are not yet very sure of ourselves.

Some might be thinking: We cannot continue this practice in our normal, everyday life. We would simply answer: Neither will you be able to pray in your everyday life as you do during the retreat. In neither case should you try to amass a spiritual capital to be used later, but rather to give yourself to the Holy Spirit, in the sharing as in the prayer, and to derive the benefits these have to offer. This experience of love, engaged in for its own sake and ultimately incommunicable, changes our way of looking at life and our ordinary relationships. Similarly, after the sharing in the Eucharist, life has not changed from what it was before; but we are no longer the same.

4. *The Daily Examen*

The examen is closely related to the spiritual dialogue, as it is to the fraternal sharing and, indeed, to the whole of a person's experience. It helps us maintain a spiritual readiness in the very midst of our life-situation. It is not self-analysis or introversion or a desire to find fault with everything, but rather an opening of our whole self to the breath of God. There we seek to recognize better the action of the Spirit, by first making an act of thanksgiving and then inquiring where our heart may have shut itself up.

Concretely, the following questions can help us take our bearings each day:

1) Questions concerning prayer: choice of a time of day, fidelity, position, satisfaction, lights, difficulties. To what did I feel moved? What worked best for me?

2) Questions concerning the atmosphere of the day: fatigue,

restlessness, distraction; joy, peacefulness, silence of the heart; the state of my habitual thoughts; the use of my time.

3) Also, those things that have to do with my health. Nothing is inconsequential for the experience under way.

Naturally, I am preoccupied with certain questions. In this silence, they come back to me, perhaps harass me. How should I deal with them? Some people, on principle, chase them away as obstacles. Others insist that they cannot pray without them. As a matter of fact, we should perform a discernment with them as starting points. It is more a matter of how we live these questions than of finding an immediate solution for them.

THE SPIRIT OF A SCHEDULE

Even a person who makes his retreat alone should decide on certain set times in the day, if only those of meals, the Eucharist, and rising. All the more so if it is a group retreat.

A conflicting, twofold requirement governs the organization of time: on the one hand, fidelity to prayer; everything is arranged to favour it. On the other hand, flexibility and freedom, so that each person can discover his own rhythm. The sign of a good schedule is that it favours fidelity while preserving peace. Having found such a schedule, why should I change it? Habits are good, if they help a person give himself more fully.

Here, by way of mere suggestion, is a schedule that I have often used in group retreats:

9.30   Laudes. Conference
12.30   Lunch
6.30   Eucharist, with a homily
7.30   Supper
8.30   Vespers, with some suggestions for the next day's prayer

The fraternal sharing can be scheduled forty-five minutes before the Eucharist. All the rest is for the individual to determine.

In a group retreat, it is good to form several teams for the preparation of the Office and the Eucharist. Besides, these teams contribute to the fraternal atmosphere so valuable for prayer.

A deep bond soon begins to be felt among those who agree to live together in silence in order to find the Lord. Far from being a burden, silence becomes the atmosphere in which the individual feels united with the others in the same Spirit. Even the person who decides not to join in the sharing does not remain isolated.

Without a doubt, we are then experiencing the very foundation of any community of Jesus's disciples. Secret ties are woven between people who as late as yesterday did not know one another.

Should the retreatants be silent at meals? Silence does not seem artificial, except for those who still find the retreat itself a burden. For the others, it is a need. Naturally, the silence can become tense if the meal is too drawn out or poorly organized. These are important details. A reading, accompanied by music, can help preserve without stress this atmosphere of relaxed and freely accepted silence.

SOME HELPS FOR THE PRAYER OF THE DAYS TO COME

1. *The Place of Prayer: The Heart (Mt. 6:5–15)*

Withdraw into that secret place, known to you alone. Do not seek to make yourself noticed, to play a role, or to repeat ready-made formulas. Be yourself before your Father, who knows the secret of your heart. Prayer is an act of a free being who assumes his proper place before God and others.

2. *A Preliminary Attitude: The Burning Bush (Ex. 3:1–20)*

In the presence of God, who is revealing himself to you as the unquenchable fire, do not try to force things, to take care of things by yourself. Take your shoes off. No one grasps God; he reveals himself, as happens when two persons let themselves be known by one another. Thus, you will come to know him in his mystery, beyond everything you can tag with a name; and then he will clothe you with your mission. Go find Pharaoh. I will be the words on your lips.

3. *Faith in Asking (Lk. 11:9-15)*

With this attitude, you will be able to ask for whatever your heart desires. How can the Father refuse you the Good Spirit if you ask him for it? For, within us who can only ask to pray properly, the Spirit utters ineffable groans (Rm. 8:26–7).

Pray to the Spirit, and he will create in you the desire for these things.

4. *Pondering the Word in Our Heart*

The believer remembers the word and repeats it to himself: the memory of the heart. "Inscribe my precepts on the tablets of your heart" (Proverbs 7:3).

I have not forgotten your Word (Ps. 119[118]).

He ponders it within himself, in order to learn Wisdom and there find his delight: the heart is the place of understanding (the whole Psalm 119[118]).

The Exercises *invite a person to remember, reflect, and then exercise his will. This is the normal rhythm of the prayer that is schooled in Scripture. There we find the taste of things.*

5. *To Whom Does God Communicate His Wisdom?*

To those who recognize its source (Bar. 3 to 4:4).
To those who ask for it: the prayer of Solomon to ask for Wisdom (Wisdom 8:17 to 9).

To the little ones (Lk. 10:21-2).
To open hearts: the sower (Lk. 8:4-15).
To those who live in fraternal love (Mt. 5:23-4; and the
Cenacle: Acts 1:12-14).

*"Watch out how you listen" (Lk. 8:18). The Exercises propose a way
of readying oneself for God's gifts.*

I. Prelude and Foundation: The Plan of God and the Response of Man

THE PURPOSE OF THE DAY: WHERE TO BEGIN?

Where should we begin? We have to start somewhere, even though today any choice of starting point might seem arbitrary and questionable. Everyone argues about the method to follow in approaching God, whether from God to the world or from the world to God. The danger is that, out of a desire to respect the approach of others, we would waste our time in discussions. Now, there is no time to waste (Rm. 13:11–12). We must get down to the essential.

There is a fundamental attitude, without which nothing is genuine in my plans or actions. This attitude lies beneath and beyond our usual contrasts of prayer and action, interiority and exteriority, as well as the contrasts that life creates among us – those of professions, social classes, educations.

This attitude is that of a freedom that consents to existence. Not a freedom that chooses things according to its own fancies, but a freedom which, recognizing its determinations and limits, accepts itself and the whole world from that love which made this freedom exist and outside of which it could not develop.

There is something unique in this consent, as there is in the "yes" of love between two persons. No one can say it for me. I myself cannot say it without descending into the depths of my being, where I am alone before God, "where the Father sees in secret". It is in this secret depth that my existence finds its unity and, at the same time, where I find my unity with all men. There I exclude nothing and no one.

It is in this consent that I begin to relativize things (that is, to refuse to isolate things as though they were absolutes) and begin rather to see them within the relationship that makes them exist. In this way I can accept them in freedom and use them in love.

35

Thus, I discover the law of all life: self-fulfilment in sharing. No one has his centre or his goal in himself. This is true for mankind as a whole as well as for the individual man. Man cannot become himself except in relation. Being is a gift, a communication.

The perfection of the world can be realized only if each person is faithful to this principle: as he goes through life, to freely descend into the depths and solitude of being and there to discover his solidarity with all beings and his total dependence upon God. What gives a human life its worth is not the accomplishment of great tasks, nor the reputation that surrounds it, nor health, riches, or long years; rather, it is the freedom which, in the situation it finds itself in, in the today whose tomorrow rests uncertain, receives itself from God in the present moment and freely opens itself to love. There begins the fullness of life.

Isn't this aspiration a dream? To leave the realm of theory, I would have to move my centre outside myself and make the other the rule of my life and choices. A liberating break would be necessary, one that makes me accept as a living truth that law of the Gospel: whoever loses his life finds it. The law of love is the acceptance of death. Then everything would be simple. Yet that is precisely what is so difficult, so impossible.

In fact, it is Christ alone who can accomplish this desire within us. That is why it is he who accomplishes and makes possible the transfiguration of the world. He lives his humanity in the freedom of love. Each desire of his heart is oriented towards accomplishing the will of the Father. He is driven by that desire; he lives by it; and because of it he dies in that human existence of his which was doomed to be short, because he had such an urgent desire that all be accomplished. However, he leaves us his Spirit, so that this urgent work begun by him can continue in us, slowly, across the centuries. The whole spiritual life consists in assimilating in our small human lives that profound orientation of the heart of Christ. Thus, in me as in him, the transfiguration of myself and of the world continues.

In order to accomplish this work, he proposed the law that he himself followed, that of renunciation. Not an ascetical renunciation that is mere privation or contempt for things. How could he who made those things demand that we flee from them? Rather, it is an openness to the love that beckons to us beyond all things. It is that which St. Ignatius describes in the following way at the beginning of his *Exercises*: "To desire and choose solely that which better leads us to the end for which we have been created." His expression is merely a translation of the exigency of life and of love. Come, follow me. If you want to build a tower, sit down first of all. Ask yourself if you have sunk good foundations, so that you will be able to carry your project through to completion (Lk. 14:25–33).

These fundamental truths, which constitute the law of existence, are thrown into a new perspective by faith. We can even ask if, without faith, they could be seen by us in such clear light. They make us return to God's original plan for man: "God created man in his image and likeness." How could man understand himself apart from him who is the Image of the Father? It is in him that we are created and understand what we are.

Revelation places us before the universal law, that of the Love which creates and which communicates itself. It is the same with the mystery of God – Father, Son, and Holy Spirit. It is the same with Christ, who lives only for his Father. It is the same with the Church, which lives only through Christ. It is the same with man and woman. It is the same with all mankind. The fulfilment of *any* person is possible only in the recognition of the other, in the radical renunciation of self. It is the nothing that opens itself to the all.

So, I launch out; and faith tells me what an adventure I am involved in. In this light, I can at least ask myself several questions so that I won't lose my way. In fact, one question is enough. In everything that happens to me, do I remain free enough to love? Put negatively: in many things, I still experience in myself fear, constraint, irritation, cowardice. I experience my limits. Do I at least agree to objectify that which is enslaving me and then, without hardening myself, remain open to the light? What will come of it? I do not know. I accept the fact that I do not know and agree to remain without defences or preconceived ideas.

From such a starting point, everything is possible; for the essential thing is in order. Do not try to escape reality – that of the world or that of yourself. You would like things to be different from what they are. You would like to be different from what you are. In order to change yourself and those things, you must first of all accept the real state of affairs. This reality will then seem relative to you; that is, it will find its sense in another reality. Then you will begin to walk without fear, because you will have begun to recognize yourself as free to love in the real world.

You see, it is not a question of denying anything in your life or of denying your ordinary concerns, but rather of descending a bit more into those depths where you encounter creative love.

– But what you are proposing here at the outset is perfection itself!

– True, but in the form of a seed. Everything is contained in this starting point, but we must let it unfold in experience in order to understand what it contains. Everything is already there in the present; yet everything remains to be done.

At every stage of my life, I can return to this foundation. Its truth takes on ever greater value with each new experience that I freely accept. I always return to the same starting point, and each time I discover it anew.

Having arrived at this summit of perfection, I must still turn loose of the satisfaction I experience; otherwise I will compromise the balance I think I have reached. This balance is maintained only by advancing. Whoever stops to look at himself will fall. I can gain nothing unless I lose more.

These truths must be mulled over. As soon as they are no longer merely an object of consideration or of discussion, they pass into the heart and become inexhaustible. Then everything changes, and everything becomes possible. Life begins to circulate – that of the Spirit, of whom "you do not know whence he comes nor where he goes" (Jn. 3:8). You know only that he is there and that he is driving you forward.

Some Helps for Today's Prayer

Each text, with its brief commentary, clarifies one aspect of the orientation of this day's prayer. Their variety permits a choice that corresponds better to the needs of the individual.

Before entering into prayer, it is good to settle upon one of these texts, so that we know where to begin. It is useless to worry about the others, if we have found what we are looking for. The others, if necessary, can be used for reading during the course of the day, as long as we do not forget that "the soul is not satisfied and filled by knowing a lot of facts but by feeling and tasting things in the depths of the heart" (Ex. 2).

1. God's Creative Presence in the Present (Ps. 138–139): *Yahweh, you probe me and you know me. . . .*

This God that we seek "is not far from any of us" (Acts 17: 22–31). He is more intimate to me than I am to myself, at the heart of each activity, enabling me to exist, to will and to act (vv. 1–6).

The more I descend into the depths of my being, the more I discover the Spirit who reaches from one end of the world to the other and whom nothing escapes (Wisdom 7:22–8:1), not even darkness or sin.

The God who at each instant gives me to myself binds me to all the other beings of the universe (vv. 7–12). He has bound us all together in love. Because he has made us, it is out of love: If you had hated anything, you would not have formed it (Wisdom 11:21–12:2). I feel myself overwhelmed by that love which does not cease to create me and which is reality itself (vv. 13–18).

This love, in which I find myself existing, I desire in its entirety. May I never be one of those who "consider your thoughts insignificant" and who want "to serve two masters" (Mt. 6:24; vv. 19–22).

Thus, in this freedom that I receive from God, I freely consent to existence. I want to stand completely unveiled before him, like the Virgin who says her *"fiat"* (vv. 23–4).

This psalm is a starting point and constitutes an entire spiritual attitude, that of the creature before his creator. In order for that attitude to become our own, there is nothing we can do but read and re-read it, to learn it by heart, in such a way that we come to re-create it within ourselves.

2. *The Genesis of the Universe and of Man: (Gen. 1 and 2)*

If we choose these two chapters to help our prayer, the important thing is to allow the fundamental attitudes involved there to take shape within ourselves, under the movement of the Spirit.

– First of all, the universe.

Everything there is the work of his Word and his love.

His word, which never returns to him who utters it without having produced its effect (Is. 50:10–11) and which "re-creates the heart" of him who entrusts himself to this word (Ps. 51[50]:12). "If you have faith, you will say to this mountain . . ." (Mt. 21:18–22).

His love, which wishes not evil but rather life for that which it creates. As though the universe, contemplated in faith, were an invitation to praise God and to thank him. The wisdom books and the Psalms develop this invitation; for example: Proverbs 8; Sirach 39:12–35; Sirach 42:15–43; Ps. 103 and 104; Job 38–42.

This universe is just the beginning of the work. There will come a new earth and a new heaven (Apoc. 21).

– Man at the centre of the universe.

This universe is entrusted to man, the image of God, so that he can exercise his freedom and, in transforming the universe, can become a co-worker of God. There is a special way in which man resembles God. For, just as God's unity is not solitude but mutual respect in love, so also man becomes himself only by understanding himself as "man and woman" and by refusing to isolate himself.

Genesis merely presents a few starting points. The rest of Scripture, and especially the coming of him who is the image of the Father – the Word made flesh – will reveal what remains hidden. Man recognizes himself only in Christ, "in whom we are transformed into that ever-more-glorious Image" (2 Cor. 3:18–4:6) and in whom we form "the new man who is making his way towards true knowledge, by renewing himself in the image of his creator" (Col. 3:10–11).

Perhaps these texts are so well known that we do not need to re-read them. If so, we should close the book and let ourselves be impregnated by the reality which the texts suggest. If we do re-read them, let this be according to faith, and not according to what is obvious to the senses. They are an invitation to read the universe and mankind the way God sees them — without despairing of his work, despite the evil that has sprung up there.

This reading can be grounded only in the prayer of the believer. That is why it is so naturally developed in the psalms of praise and adoration.

3. The Revelation of the Mystery

These fundamental truths can be deepened under different aspects. Many texts can help in this. The best are those which each person discovers for himself. Here are some that develop one point or another connected with this Foundation.

We receive each one of these texts as a burning residue from a spiritual experience undergone by the apostles John and Paul. We ask that we ourselves may be admitted into this experience, to the extent that the Spirit permits this.

The Plan of God: The Mystery of Christ (Eph. 1)

This hymn of benediction explicitates what the work of the six days contained in seed: all men coming into divine sonship in Christ. This loving plan, which is being accomplished throughout all the ages and which joins visible and invisible beings together in love, takes place in each of us through the Word we have received and through the Spirit poured into our hearts. God opens the eyes of our heart so that we can see the extraordinary grandeur of our destiny and grasp the magnitude of our hope.

Our Life in the Spirit (Jn. 14)

Another way to penetrate the mystery of our divine destiny is to understand God's gift of the Holy Spirit, who is given to us by the Son. There is a presence more extraordinary than the visible presence of the Word-made-flesh among men, and that is the Lord's presence through the gift of his Spirit. A permanent presence which illumines us with truth and, especially, which makes us enter into the intimacy of God. This presence takes shape in the heart that has become God-like through the life of the commandments, and it produces a peace over which the world has no control.

The Life in the Freedom of the Sons of God (Rm. 8)

There is still another aspect of our life in the Spirit, that of liberation. We are acquainted with the sufferings of the present time; but, through the Spirit who testifies to our spirit that we are sons, we know where these sufferings are leading us. Our redemption and that of the universe are accomplished against the backdrop of the groans of our waiting. We can also work right now with confidence. For those who love him, God is at work in everything, to bring them to that perfect image. Even the tribulations of the present world, even all the hostile things in the universe – tribulation, anguish, death – cannot separate us from the love of God, who through Christ has manifested himself within us.

God in the Reality of Love (1 Jn. 4:7-16)

Out experience of love on earth constitutes for us both the rough sketch of the knowledge of God and also its ultimate manifestation; for whoever loves is born of God and knows God. As John says in Chapter 2 of the same epistle, the new commandment of brotherly love incorporates the old commandment received in the very beginning, according to which man should love his fellow man like himself. It is in the reality of this love that I run up against the reality of God, who is love. If we love one another, God remains in us; in us his love is realized.

There is nothing more to say about God once we have said he is Love – that is, gratuity, initiative, sharing. God is the first to love. He creates, and he re-creates that which is deformed, so that, in his Christ, all men can participate in his Spirit. Thus, in the love from which they live, they will know that God exists. Not the love we try to produce in our own hearts by sheer will-power but that love with which God loves himself and us and which he communicates to us.

The brotherly community in the Church is the privileged place for this presence of God-love. It is in and from the Church that love spreads out to all men and returns to the Father. Again, though, we must add with St. John that "The Spirit breathes where he will" (Jn. 3:8).

The Two States of Our Destiny (1 Jn. 3:1–3)

Our existence as God's children, which separates us from a world enclosed within itself and wanting to live solely on its own resources, is lived by us in two ways: in reality and in hope. "Beginning now" we are children of God; but this reality is possessed only as a sacrament: what we are has not yet been manifested. Here, where we exist in time, we are being educated in faith.

Yet "we know", with a certitude produced in us by the "unction" of the Spirit (1 Jn. 2:27) and more solid than the data of our senses or the reasoning of our mind, that this perfect resemblance will come "when he will appear".

To see him will transform us into him. This will be the perfect knowledge: I will know as I am known (1 Cor. 13:12).

The secret of all human perfection is there: the hope Jesus gives us for our total transfiguration. Then the meaning of our creation will appear in the image of our creator.

The meditation on our destiny, whatever text we choose, should develop into an intimate conversation, "like a friend speaking to his friend"

43

(Ex. 54). Finally, this prayer can be nourished by praying the Office or the Psalms; a word, a verse, or a phrase can help me relish throughout the day that which the meditation has helped me penetrate. In this way the Word of God becomes flesh and life in me.

4. *The Gift of My Heart*

I can see where today's prayer is leading me: Love him who made you (Sirach 7:30).

Hence, I should come "to desire and choose solely that which better leads me to the purpose for which I am created" (*Ex.* 23). If this purpose is the total transformation of existence, I should offer myself to this transformation with both the rigour of the evangelical ideal and the circumspection of one who considers whether he has the means to carry out his undertaking (Lk. 14:25–33).

I can close this prayer with Psalm 39–40: You have done marvels for us. You have not desired sacrifices. I said: here I am to do your will. I have taken pleasure in your law in the very depths of my heart. May your love preserve me.

This first day can give us some idea of how to use Scripture in our prayer. The essential thing is to try to develop the disposition that was indicated as the object of the present day. Each person chooses the texts which best correspond to the goal he has set; and, if he finds in these texts what he wants, he should not worry about finding any other.

DISCERNMENT AT THE END OF THE DAY

At the end of the first day, we should be able to turn the page, without, however, failing to note the results. It is a question of a subsequent reflection on what has happened – not for the pleasure of analysis, not to become discouraged, but to profit from everything, even from our mistakes.

One point that is good to examine is the quality of our

silence. If someone has not achieved a silence that is both integral and (especially) peaceful, we might wonder if he is mature enough for the experience he is engaged in. Tension and fatigue – except for the fatigue normal for the first day – are never good signs. If we experience them, these dispositions reveal obstacles that we are putting in the way of the Spirit's action. In this case, we must know how to change our procedure. Such a person, who may have decided to let nothing slip by, should admit his need to relax. It is better to do less with joy than a lot with tenseness.

Submission to the hour of prayer teaches me not to seek mere sentiments or ideas in prayer, but rather fidelity and desire. Take me with you for the glory of the Father. The *Exercises* will lead us to pray thus to Jesus, when we reach their summit, the meditation of the Standards. This is present in germ from the very beginning. Sometimes I finish, happy with the past hour; sometimes I think I have wasted my time. I should become neither conceited about success nor discouraged by failure. I should not resign myself to my hardness, my dryness, or my distractions as if they were inevitable; rather, I should move on without panicking. I go to prayer for God, waiting upon him for the outcome, however and whenever I am allowed to attain this.

I can flee from this experience by distracting myself, by chatting. But there is a more subtle way of doing it: I can get myself all comfortably set up in the retreat. Thus, I dodge the necessity of prayer by reading spiritual books or entertaining beautiful and generous ideas which have nothing to do with the task at hand. I take copious notes and develop all sorts of ideas. In this way, I run away from the work of the Holy Spirit to a task set by my own mind. I keep running into myself instead of losing myself. It helps to objectify in oneself the attractiveness of this temptation. We experience this same temptation in certain times of dryness and agitation.

The proposed way of praying constitutes a concrete introduction into the life of faith. Prayer becomes an experiment in which I discover what I am and the degree of grace that God is granting to me. "Another" (the Spirit) is leading me; and I try to submit myself to his always-unpredictable action. The examen of conscience then becomes an act of "gratefully recognizing" the action of God at the very heart of my day. That is how

45

I can make the examen beginning this evening. Afterwards I will continue to make it this way.

There is another way of submitting myself to the action of the Spirit. I come into the retreat with the problems and difficulties in my life. My submission to the object of my prayer forces me, not to ignore these problems or to flee from them, but to put them in their place. Thus prayer, by purifying and illuminating my heart, leads me to the point where I can judge these problems with greater honesty and sense the direction in which God is drawing me. This will happen when God wants, not when I want.

Little by little, I discover what generosity means. It does not suppose that I achieve results immediately and through my own efforts — especially the results as *I* imagine them. Rather, it demands that I begin the journey again and again with increased confidence. A struggle is necessary to hold my attention, but violence is out of place; we need peace of mind in order to enter into prayer.

I am constantly navigating between two reefs. The first is that of pure spontaneity. I take what I want. I remain the plaything of my impulses, of the wake of my feelings or actions, of the impressions I make (or think I make) on others. This is a false independence. The second reef is the opposite of the first; it is that of pure will-power. I want to succeed, and I am never at ease. After some time, I cannot hold on any longer; I become discouraged and give up the ship. Instead of trying to hold on at all costs and in the most rigid way possible, I would do better to relax and sleep. God will take good care of "his beloved who is sleeping" (Ps. 127[126]:2).

These notes, portraying various possible reactions, should prime us for a spiritual dialogue. I do not expect the director to tell me what I should do; rather, as I express myself in his presence, he should help me interpret these movements that I am beginning to feel — or not to feel. Then I will see this dialogue as a gradual formation in docility to the Spirit, through a freedom that seeks to open itself to grace.

FIRST STAGE:
The Call to Conversion

By living it himself, Jesus reveals to us the ideal whose imprint we already carry, though in a confused and clouded manner. At the same time, he reveals to us the evil in which we are immersed and out of which he is leading us. He becomes the only one who can help us reach our goal. Despite his solidarity with our life and our death, he is the revelation of the Image of God, in which we are created.

It is therefore his presence in us that leads us to the first stage of every spiritual life, conversion of heart. The Jews, abruptly confronted with the marvels of Pentecost, asked Peter and the apostles, who had just told them about these marvels: "Brothers, what must we do?" Love, in manifesting itself, highlights the darkness from which it delivers us. Touched in his depths by this love, man longs for a justice that comes, not from himself, but from God who justifies the sinner.

We are speaking of stages. In the actual unfolding of experience, we should speak rather about the mutual inclusion of the various stages. We cannot separate one from the other, the knowledge of Jesus from the knowledge of ourselves. Though the person examining the matter from the outside sees successive notions, the person living it within his heart discovers the continuity of the Spirit's work. There can be no successful purgative phase unless Christ is already present in the glory of his Resurrection.

The more a person advances in Christ, the more this continuity makes itself felt. The most intimate friends of Christ insist they are the greatest sinners. At first, we make the two opposites. That shows that we still have a long way to go in the spiritual life. Little by little, everything becomes a whole.

The entrance into this stage is, therefore, an invitation to sense both the call of life and also the force of gravity that prevents from responding to it. The search for love reveals the resistance in myself: I do not do the good I want but the evil I do not want. I am divided, and all mankind along with me. Who will deliver me? I cannot escape from this division unless Jesus puts me back together. I cannot escape from the hell in which I discover myself unless Jesus descends there with me and leads me back with him towards the Father.

II.   In the Depths

Its goal is to situate us before the reality of sin. On our own, we are incapable of grasping the depths of sin. To descend there, we need the light of Revelation. What does it tell us?

Sin is the will to credit myself alone with the fulfilment of my existence; it is the refusal to situate myself before God and others in a relationship of love, the rejection of all dependence, and the persistence in the solitude of self. In another way, it is the act of freedom which isolates itself or which hesitates to open itself. St. Ignatius says that it is "the refusal to use one's freedom to give respect and obedience to our Creator and Lord" (*Ex.* 50).

This evil is not an individual affair. It is a state of intimate division in which I find myself involved along with all other men. There I am torn between two inclinations: that of light and love which call to me from above, that of "my evil heart" which drags me downward. Depending upon the choice of my heart, I become what I want to be.

Thus, the knowledge I am seeking is not first of all the knowledge of my own skin. I would still be able to make comparisons and think that I am better than others. Rather, it is the knowledge of an evil in which all of us are immersed, a radical and universal evil.

Our text presents this state to us in different degrees. According to the plan of the first meditation of the *Exercises*, it is found in its pure state in "the sin of the Angels". Certain people today are ill at ease with this account. Yet, especially if we understand it in the light of Scripture, it at least has the advantage of confronting us with the ultimate content of any sin: not forgetfulness or an act of weakness, but a refusal to live and to love, a sort of ontological monstrosity that turns the world upside down.

Although this pride is the root of evil, our experience is more

49

at home with the second and third sins, that of Adam and Eve and that of the unnamed man. It is no longer sin in its pure state, but the subterfuge of a heart that stakes its well-being on something other than the essential. The long human history is made up of ambiguous desires, incapacitating fears, self-seeking, ill-directed instincts, fickle thoughts. Freedom, which feels the dead-weight of the self, sets out on side-roads. Like Narcissus, it gazes at itself and wants to find its joy in itself; but it then discovers that it is all alone.

Sin is not considered to be primarily an infraction of the law. No doubt, a law is given to me, whether a written law or a law of the conscience; but, in so far as it remains external to me, I can judge it and be judged by it. Thus, it leaves me to myself, far from God. I must delve deeper if I want to discover the ultimate evil, where divisions arise in the heart of a person and among persons. The law can be given to me, to help me discover this ultimate evil; but, faithful or unfaithful to this law, I cannot discover in it the righteousness to which I aspire. It abandons me to my own powerlessness. Only in Jesus, who assumes in his flesh the condemnation of the law, does the wall of separation fall and the law become interior to me.

As I discover this state of sin, I simultaneously discover Christ at the roots of my being. He bridges the gap that separates us from him; he comes with us into the absence of God. Creator, he made himself man; immortal, he experiences death. Being with us in the midst of evil, he delivers us from it, as soon as we recognize him as our only Saviour, who makes possible the sharing of love between God and ourselves – a love without which we could not exist.

Thus, more than my ignorance or weakness, what I primarily want to discover in this frank meditation is how I develop the interior attitude that makes me the centre and makes me see things only in relation to myself. This is what cuts me off from love and, therefore, from life. In the end, the tree falls in the direction it has been leaning; and my heart finds what it has been desiring – myself or Christ. "If I had not come, they would have had no sin." But the light must come, and everyone must declare what he wants.

By revealing us as devoid of love, this day tries to make us accept the salvation offered by Jesus Christ. In this descent to the heart of evil, I do not allow myself to judge others. It is my evil that I want to come to know. I ask for "shame and confusion about myself" in that "exile" of which I am so unaware. It is to this evil that Christ awakens me and from which, being enclosed with us there, he delivers me.

The "Meditation"

Our purpose calls for a special way of meditating, that of a faith that receives its light from God. It is this method that we should use each time we open the Scripture. Like the young girl who represents the contemplative life on the tympanum of Chartres' north portal, whoever meditates should sit quietly, open the book, read a passage, repeat in his heart the words he has read, and then enter into ecstasy. Then he can move into the active life.

This is the rhythm proposed by the *Exercises*. First I place before my heart's memory the fact of sin, just as the faith hands it down to me. It has a history that extends far beyond myself (an "invisible reality", says St. Ignatius) – something I did not create, yet into which I find myself inserted. It is the history of that sin whose source is even more distant and more powerful, a history whose foundation Christ attributes to Satan.

Then I consider this history the best I can. Not so much with the discursive intellect, which analyses, discusses, and proves, but with the pondering intellect, which the wisdom books mention. I search for comparisons, connections, and examples that clarify what I want to understand. It is an effort of spiritual understanding, beginning with the data of faith. Through this effort, as St. Paul says (Col. 2:2), "we come to the full development of that understanding that helps us penetrate the mysteries of God". Faith then becomes a living wisdom.

Then the heart rests in the enjoyment of the truth. For the moment, it feels no need to continue its search. Closing the book, a person lets the light he has received become penetrated with love. Thus, the truth passes from the head to the heart. "Not too high, not too low," said one retreatant; "I had been locating my prayer either in ideas or else in gut feelings – and not in the heart." The liturgy follows the same movement: it reads, it explains, it delights in the Word.

To do this is undoubtedly to rediscover the meaning of the "*lectio divina*". This traditional way of reading Scripture tries primarily, not to do an exegesis of it, but to discover – through the words used, the thoughts developed, the facts written about – the invisible reality they all lead to but which surpasses them all. There the heart opens itself to the light, in the presence of the Word that reveals us to ourselves and reveals God to us in faith. Through the effects it produces in us, this Word shows that the Holy Spirit is its origin.

HELPS FOR TODAY'S PRAYER

Before entering into prayer, it is good to ready oneself, not only by focusing one's mind on a subject (a particular text of Scripture) but in establishing a fitting atmosphere. The spiritual authors, St. Igantius included, speak of preludes for prayer. Here, then, first of all, are two texts that can help to put us in the right mood before meditating on the nature of sin.

1. *The Mood of These Meditations*

Peter's Bewilderment (Lk. 5:1–11)

Meeting God in Jesus brings with it a deeper revelation of self.

Both aspects prepare a person to enter more fully into his vocation. The light reveals the darkness; and the darkness, where I recognize what I am, makes me feel the need for the light. Thus I can accept with peace the mission that is mine.

Peter, who already lives in intimacy with Jesus, suddenly discovers him as his creator, the Almighty God, the source of each Word and of all marvels.

At that moment, the person reels. He does not know what to say, what to do. He is dazed. He recognizes simultaneously God and his own interior division: "Depart from me, Lord, because I am a sinner!" How is it that you, the Completely Other, bring yourself so close?

It is in this moment of truth that we become capable of receiving our mission: "Be confident; you shall become a fisher of men." With the same motion in which you throw yourself at my feet, you are given to men. The word that you will transmit to them will be my word upon your lips.

Everything is given at the same time: creation, bewilderment, vocation.

We could add: it is given to the companions of the Lord. They no longer have any interest in comparing themselves with one another, at least not now. The Lord is the focal point of their vision. It is in him that they recognize themselves.

The Prayer of Baruch, or the Exiles' Prayer (Bar. 1:15–3:8)

This is the composition of place for the prayer of the sinner. At the same time, it guarantees the genuineness of this prayer, focusing (as in the bewilderment of Peter) our gaze on God and making us judge things in relation to him.

Sin is a state of absence, of exile: "the whole human composite", says Ignatius (*Ex.* 47), "is as though it were exiled". I am far from my homeland, outside life, in a state of division and death – and it does not even seem to bother me. One need only take a look at the human condition.

The evil comes from the fact that I seek for righteousness where it is not to be found, apart from God: I have sought to justify myself by my own efforts, and I have achieved nothing but shame as a result. Myself and all of us, we are outside the truth.

What should I accuse myself of? "We have not listened to the voice of the Lord" – at least not very often. "We have set out, each one following the inclination of his wicked heart" (1:22). "We have not begged the Lord's mercy to turn each of us away from the thoughts of his wicked heart" (2:8). Like those invited to the wedding, we had something else to do, always something else to do. Following the inclinations of a self that desires nothing but itself, we have become that towards which our heart was leading us: the solitary self, the hell of a man wrapped up in himself. Sensing my hard heart, I did not turn it towards the Lord so that he could soften it. With God absent, there reigned hardness, hatred, foolishness. "And so the Lord kept watch over these calamities . . ." (2:9).

The one who rediscovers life is not the person who lies complacently in this death (2:17) but rather the person "who sets out before the Lord", just as he is, "stooped and without strength, with failing eyes and a hungry soul" (2:18). God draws good out of this excess of evil. The person, "coming back to his senses" (2:30), recognizes the Lord and "remembers his father's house" (Lk. 15:17). God gives him a heart and ears. From a "crushed heart" he creates a "new heart" (Ps. 51[50]), capable of loving. The law becomes interior to him.

God's way of drawing a man out of his exile consists in giving him his Spirit through the cross of his Son: "How is it that he, the creator, ever decided to become man?" (*Ex.* 53).

2. *The Revelation of Sin*

All of Scripture, by revealing God in Jesus Christ, reveals to us the sin from which Jesus frees us. In order to penetrate the nature of this evil, let us follow the stages of its history, as these are presented in the Exercises.

The Sin of Satan (Jn. 8)

The history begins beyond the world of man. It is of "an invisible realm" (*Ex.* 47) and begins with him who did not want to remain in the power that he had received in the beginning,

54

but who left his proper home (Jude 6) – Satan, the father of evil, as Christ calls him.

Chapter 8 of John's Gospel helps us penetrate the nature of Satan's sin by contrasting the sons of God, freed by the Son, and the sons of the devil, who fulfil the desires of their father. On the one hand, transparency, truth, relationship, life, a continual reference to the Father, freedom in love; on the other hand, enclosure within oneself, refusal to recognize the other, absence of relationships, lies, solitude, division. A person is real and free only if he recognizes in his heart the relationship that makes him exist: as the Son before the Father, we are ourselves only in relationship with all those from whom we receive our existence or with whom we share it.

Suddenly, sin appears in its profound nature: the refusal of the relationship that makes a person exist and establishes him in love. It is the inclination of the heart that causes sin: you become the son of the one you have decided to resemble. If you accept the word of the Son, then you recognize the truth and the truth makes you free. If you shut yourself up within your privileges – even if it be your claims to be a son of Abraham or a son of God – despite your pretention, your desire becomes that of a son of the devil, who enclosed himself in himself and in death. Through his word, Jesus reveals to us the sources of both life and death.

The Sin of Adam and Eve (Genesis 3)

It is the beginning of human history. The man created in the image of God distances himself from his creator. He wants to decide for himself what is good and bad; making himself the centre, he cuts himself off from others. He hides himself from God, who has suddenly become distant. He wants to dominate the other person whom the creator has given him, while the woman tries to seduce her companion. Something is rending asunder at the very heart of the universe.

This story, which we locate at the beginning of mankind, could be located perhaps better at the beginning of my acts. "Every-one plays god when he says: 'This is good' or 'This is bad', or when he derives excessive joy or sadness from events" (Pascal). Man wants to be the measure of himself and of all things.

This is the precise sin of the man who, receiving the blessings and the promise of God, argues and murmurs. God cannot give us anything to drink in this desert, say the sons of Israel to Moses. They have forgotten the God who has been saving them, as the Psalms and the Prophets repeat again and again. Thus, there is not one who seeks God (Ps. 53[52]). They have gone astray from the womb (Ps. 58[57]). It is a generation that totally lacks a steadfast heart (Ps. 78[77]). A confession of the sins of the whole people (Ps. 106[105]). With what should I compare this generation, says Jesus. We played the flute, and you would not dance. We intoned a song of mourning, and you would not weep (Mt. 11:16–17). Him who invited you to the wedding feast you have countered with refusal, inattention, and forget-fulness (the parables). A straying, heedless, obstinate heart. You have turned away from me, the source of living waters, repeat the prophets (Jer. 1 to 11). With the coming of Jesus, this sin of the self-enclosed man bursts into full light.

The Sin of All Humanity: Pagans and Jews (Rm. 1 to 11)

This sin, which is the diversion towards oneself of the inclination that draws each person towards love, has swept over humanity. Whoever we are, pagans or Jews, we must recognize that we are imprisoned there: the pagan, who, in the midst of creation, does not recognize his creator, but diverts things to his own profit; the Jew, who, receiving the promises and the law of God, prides himself in them and thinks that he is better than the others. Thus, "the entire world is judged guilty before God" and finds itself enclosed in wickedness and death. And whoever tries to escape through his own efforts experiences his interior divi-sion – not doing the good that he wants, doing the evil he does not want. For both pagans and Jews, there is no salvation, life, or righteousness except in the recognition of Jesus Christ, who has become our righteousness. It is in him that God extends mercy to all, tearing down every wall of separation and killing hatred (Eph. 2).

This long history, described by St. Paul, is the history of humanity; yet it is also our personal history. In myself, too, there is at times the pagan, at times the Jew. I cling to the gifts of God as though in a universe that fulfils all my needs, a universe where the self is king and death reigns.

3. *A Repetition of This Revelation in the Parable of the Two Sons (Lk. 15:11–32)*

I can re-read this parable in the light of the Letter to the Romans. There I see, one after the other, the sin of the pagan and the sin of the Jew. The sin of the prodigal who uses his freedom to hoard things is the sin of the pagan: whatever comes my way, he says, belongs to me. Thinking only of himself, he cannot help but end up in destitution. To escape from it, he must recognize the one from whom he receives everything: I will go find my Father. Once more, freedom opens itself to love. The irreproachable one, the Jew of the Letter to the Romans, is closed to this love despite his fidelity. He uses his righteousness to vindicate his rights and reject his brother. He does not understand that "everything I have is yours". To escape from sin means that, however numerous my faults, I never stop turning towards love, recognizing there the source of all good.

Both of them, the prodigal and the irreproachable, are justified only if they recognize the righteousness of the only Son, "the first-born of all creation". Though by nature equal with the Father, he became like men, making himself into sin, like them, so that he might save them all (Col. 1:15 and Phil. 2:6–8).

When a person closes himself to love, he becomes, in turn, Satan, Adam, Eve, a member of the family of sinners. When he recognizes what he is, he opens himself to love and becomes, in turn, Christ, the Virgin, a member of the family of saints.

The unfolding of our history in sin is presented to us exactly in inverse order to its unfolding in experience. At the very outset, we are lead to the heart of that invisible reality, that "proto-sin" which is at the origin of all sin and which is revealed to us by faith. In fact, we become aware of this "secret evil" (Ps. 19[18]:13) only little by little, to the extent that our freedom grows. Christ came to reveal this universal sin and to elimi-nate it. I can meditate on this history in its entirety or on one of its particular moments, according to the desire I experience. At any rate, I will not exhaust it all at one sitting.

The "depths" are revealed to me only little by little, to the extent that I can bear to look at them and to the extent that I become myself.

4. The End of This Meditation: "Colloquy", or "The Prayer to Jesus"

Everyone knows the prayer from the Eastern tradition: *Jesus, Son of God, Saviour, have pity on me, a sinner.* It contains everything and can be repeated indefinitely throughout one's whole life, without his ever being able to exhaust its truth. Jesus appears there just as he does in that conversation to which Ignatius invites the retreatant at the end of this meditation: "Imagining Christ on the cross in front of me, I will ask him why he, the creator, decided to become man; why he came from eternal life into temporal death, thus to die for my sins . . ." (*Ex.* 53).

The act that condemns me is nailed to the cross (Col. 2:14–15). There is no longer any condemnation, except for him who, placed in the presence of this mercy, refuses to recognize it.

From now on:

For him who hopes in you, there is no shame (Ps. 25[24]).
Purify me from the secret evil.
Preserve your servant from pride (Ps. 19[18]; Ps. 13[14]).

This meditation cannot leave us indifferent. If it produces nothing but boredom, this should cause some soul-searching. Usually this meditation causes what St. Ignatius, in his vocabulary, calls consolations or desolations. This language, like that concerning sin and angels, can seem obsolete. Without delaying on this point, let us try a first act of discernment.

The sense of sin has its counterfeits. Many say, "I am a lousy guy", and think that they have the sense of sin. In fact, they have the exact opposite. This sense cannot come from the Spirit if it produces sulking, discouragement, guilt feelings, comparison with others, or a morbid sadness. The feelings that have the divine trademark are strength, gentleness, the certitude of being loved by God, the desire to open myself to greater love.

Likewise, the knowledge that generates and accompanies this sense is not the result of an analysis of self or of others. It avoids all comparisons and makes us reach the depths, where we simultaneously recognize that we are incapable of good and that we are called to complete perfection. "From the depths I cry to you" (Ps. 130[129]). I cried: "the Lord saved me because he loves me" (Ps. 18[17]:20).

This is a first act of discernment accomplished by an intelligence enlightened by faith. If there are tears, they do not result from being troubled. The tears for which I may ask are a fruit of the Spirit: *educ de cordis nostri duritia lacrymas compunctionis*, a prayer in the missal used to say. My heart is as hard as a rock; make tears of compunction spring forth from it, just as water sprang forth from the rock at the prayer of Moses. These tears bring joy: "Blessed are those who weep; they shall be comforted." In contrast to the "sadness of the world" that "produces death", these tears are "the sadness from God" that "produces a saving repentance which causes no regret" (2 Cor. 7:10).

That means that this meditation can be made only by those persons who consider themselves saved in Jesus Christ. It could be harmful for those to whom Jesus Christ is not yet the one who lives in us and who re-establishes us in love; for it could enclose such people within their solitude and sadness. This is something that experience teaches the retreat director. He should show a lot of discretion in the way he presents these meditations, so as not to obtain a result opposite the one he is looking for. These meditations are bad if they do not increase in us the knowledge and love of Jesus, the Saviour.

COUNSELS AT THE END OF THE DAY

Their purpose is to help us progress in discernment, to establish us in the objective order of faith and under the action of the Holy Spirit.

1. *The Importance of the Preliminaries of Prayer*

It would be more accurate to say: the importance of starting points, of the "preludes" that set the tone.

The care we have shown for these things indicates how much importance we give to the action of the Spirit. "To ask for what I want," says St. Ignatius. Many forget one of the two parts of this directive and especially forget how important it is to take them in their correlation. I pray because, to the extent I want something to be built up or torn down within myself, I recognize how incapable I am of accomplishing it. I expect God to accomplish what he has led me to desire.

"What I want." Very frequently I do not know what I should want; I do not know what is good for me. I nevertheless request it according to the faith of the Church, knowing that God will let me see what I need, if I am trying to do my best. Through my various attempts, God will let me know what is good for me.

2. *How to Help and Maintain Ourselves in Prayer*

We should try to determine what best helps us persevere for the prescribed time – whether the Psalms or the text of Scripture and of the liturgy that support my prayer. There is something stupid and pretentious about wanting to generate everything from ourselves, since the Spirit has taken the trouble to instruct

60

us through his Word. Little by little, as the day goes on, a continuous rhythm is established in me, going from reading to prayer and from prayer to reading.

3. *Patience in Our Expectations*

Not only is this sense of sin the work of grace and not of mental tension; its revelation, in the history of mankind and of the individual man, is also progressive. That is, this revelation occurs in proportion to the strength of the person who receives it.

It is important to be contented with the degree of grace given to us today. The imagined "best" is, here as elsewhere, the enemy of the real good. To tire ourselves trying to achieve it exposes us to the discouragement that delivers us over to Satan. We should be attentive, but without haste or feverishness.

That patience is nourished by the following certitude: God reveals our wickedness to us only by giving us our Redeemer. "The fact that I tell you about it is the sign that I want to heal you from it" (Pascal).

4. *"Gathering the Fruits"*

At the end of the day, it is good to note the points that have stayed with me, if only to return to them. These are the indications of the Spirit. I might say a few words about them in the visit or in the sharing. These are also the points that sketch an orientation. Their convergence lets the will of God gradually become known, the election ultimately being merely the harvesting of a ripe fruit.

It is also good, if we seem to be getting nothing out of it, to say so. Frequently we think we are getting nothing out of it; yet, without suspecting it, grace is working in us, though in a way other than we think. As Scripture often puts it: God was there, and I was completely unaware of it.

III. The Prayer to Jesus

How can I say in truth, and not merely with my lips, the prayer to Jesus: *Jesus, son of God, Saviour, have pity on me, a sinner?*

In the very midst of the evil I find myself in, Jesus is always with me. As low as I might descend in humanity, he is there. This evening you will be with me in Paradise. With him, I go deeper than mere prohibition, to see the ugliness of sin, "even if it were not forbidden" (*Ex.* 57). Thus I arrive at the source of the common disorder, through which I, along with all men, belong to that world spoken of by St. John and from which Jesus frees me – where all justification is impossible, for the Jewish man, who judges according to the law, as well as for the pagan man, who relies upon his own conscience.

In these depths, I can condemn no one but myself. I discover the dimensions of salvation: the Breadth, the Length, the Height, and the Depth (Eph. 3:18). These are the dimensions of that love which is stronger than Hell. In the most intimate part of myself, I am in contact with the sources of eternal mercy, where Christ saves me. "Remain steadfast in the very midst of Hell and do not despair," said Jesus to the monk Silvanus of Athos. Jesus is there for me, for all men, as Saviour, as the Lamb who bears the sin of the world. He restores me to fraternal love (1 Jn. 1:8–2:2).

A sharing takes place through this encounter. I give him what I am; he gives me what he is. The transformation of man begins there. I can lay bare before him the crimes of humanity. Where sin abounds, there the grace of Jesus abounds all the more (Rm. 5).

In appropriating the prayer of the sinner, I must not fear to descend to the very bottom, to the outer limit of "the inclination of my wicked heart", into the state of pure absence, where the person who takes pleasure in himself alone sinks his roots into Hell. We must free the reality of Hell from the images we surround it with and from the questions we ask about it. Each individual bears Hell within himself; that is, a world without love, without relationships, without God. Its reality is born in us from the desire of our heart.

If I call Jesus "Saviour", I should know what he saves me from. From nothing less than Hell – the incomprehensible, the darkness, the upside-down world, the contrary of love. Sometimes here on earth I experience this state where persons, bound to themselves, remain impermeable to one another.

The descent into the very depths is not discouraging but purifying. It is the painful return of a person who is attracted by love but who feels himself resisting. By forcing this evil into the light, I escape from it. I rediscover myself in Christ, the heart of the world and of mankind. Do not cast me off far from your face. You alone are life. In you alone is the universal righteousness to which men aspire. Before, during, and after his coming upon earth, all are related to him and judged by him.

HELPS FOR TODAY'S PRAYER

1. *The Pattern of This Prayer: "Meditation on Sins" (Ex. 51–61)*

Although this is called a meditation "on sins", it is not an examination of conscience. It is a personal confrontation between God and man, along the lines of the dialogue of Job and his Creator. This meditation is composed of five large waves that wash us into the depths of mercy.

No matter how I view myself – the places where I live, my relationships, the things I do – I discover in myself the presence or the beginnings of Satan's attitude: greed and self-seeking, even in those actions which seem to be the most generous.

The malice of this attitude does not stem so much from its prohibition or from possible punishment. Even if it were not forbidden, sin – which makes me the centre – is evil, because it is the refusal to love and to live: the absolutely solitary self.

What am I, I who wish to be alone? One does not have to reflect long in order to answer the question. Corruption reaches to the very roots of such a person; and the death that awaits a man is no more than the image of the interior degradation produced in him by the self that wants to be alone.

Caught up for a moment in the wave of nothingness and despair, suddenly here I am, drawn into the more powerful wave of the God who made me. Who is he, this creator of mine? He is everything I aspire to yet cannot accomplish myself. Like Job, "I have spoken like an insane person. But now my eye has seen you. I repent in ashes and dust" (Job 42:1-6). You alone are holy. You alone are powerful. You alone are good.

And there, in the last wave, are God and man face to face in an act of "immense love". I am dazed, as was St. Peter. How is this possible? I exist. I am loved. The universe exists. The saints and angels are with me. I am not alone.

In the end, I can do nothing but converse with God our Lord: I must thank our Lord very much, concludes Ignatius. Thanksgiving follows a dynamic exactly the inverse of sin's. I am swept up into the love that creates and re-creates me.

A prayer like this is a cry, springing up from a heart to which God has revealed himself. It is beyond our power to bring it to birth at will. It is the Spirit's work within the person who asks for it: Lord, open my eyes to your marvels and I will know who I am. As it develops, it binds me indissolubly to love.

2. *A Repetition from Scripture: God's Reproaches Against Israel (Ez. 16)*

It is still the same movement: it goes from God to me, from me to God. Here it is the dialogue between a very loving husband and his unfaithful wife. Here sin appears as adultery.

In the return of man to God, it is God who takes the initiative: "Make Jerusalem know her crimes" (v. 2). "I will remember and you will remember" (vv. 60–3). Thus Jesus, after the denial of Peter, turns and gazes at his apostle. "And Peter remembered . . ." (Lk. 22:61–2).

The sin from which God draws his people is an act of ingratitude and an act of adultery. You flaunted your beauty and did not recognize that it came from me. Thus, you thought you were better than your sisters, better than Sodom, Gomorrah, and Samaria, whom you used to mock. Yet "by your abominations, you have justified your sisters" (v. 51), who have not "committed half of your crimes". St. Paul will say the same: the infidelity of Israel has justified the nations (Rm. 9 to 11).

Because you have turned away from me, I have left you to yourself. You have become the plaything of the nations. Sin has developed in you its power and deadliness: "You have delivered us over to the power of our crimes" (Isaiah 64:6). You have become an image of Hell. But my love is stronger than your crimes. I will reconcile you with myself. You will be "seized with shame", and you will no longer be tempted to consider yourself better than anyone else. Confusion, a shout of admiration, astonished silence – it is all the same thing. Man, saved with all his brothers by the universal mercy, does not know what to say: how could God have loved us so much?

In this meditation on sin in the light of Scripture, we find ourselves at a focal point which illuminates all of human history.

3. Some of the Penitents in Scripture

It is good to meditate on how God reveals sin to men and how he delivers them from it. It is always in a personal dialogue where God and man recognize one another.

David (2 Samuel 11 to 12)

Adultery, attempted corruption of the husband, murder: one sin leads to another. To become conscious of the evil into which man has sunk, the word of God must make itself heard: This man is you, says Nathan. Confronted with this word, David succumbs neither to pride nor to despair: I have sinned before God. God and man recognize one another: I have found David my servant. Saul calculates and defends himself: I have executed God's command. He denies that anything is wrong with him; he is rejected. David offers no defence; he is chosen for ever.

Zacchaeus (Lk. 19:1–10)

In the presence of Jesus, Zacchaeus recognizes that he is a thief. Roman law prescribed that a thief repay four times the stolen amount, and he promises to repay this fourfold sum. Nevertheless, though he is a publican and is known as such by all, he wants to see Jesus. Having recognized Jesus as the Unique One, he in turn is recognized by Jesus as a son of Abraham. Like Matthew and so many before him, he receives Jesus at his table, to the scandal of the Pharisees (Mt. 9:9–13).

The Sinner-Woman at Simon's Banquet (Lk. 7:36–50)

There is a danger that "descending into the depths" might mean for many people an exhaustive self-examination. The woman at Simon's banquet descended to the place where the Father sees what is hidden, and there she recognized Jesus and was recognized by him.

She says nothing; she accuses herself of nothing. Her gesture says everything. Besides, everyone in the city knows her; and the Pharisee, more than anyone else, is capable of enumerating her misdeeds. He remains within the perspectives of the Law, of quantity and of personal justification. Thus he remains alone, outside love. He has no need of anyone else. He suffices for himself.

The woman descends into herself to the point where she recognizes simultaneously that she is a sinner and that she is loved.

For her it is not a question of analysing or of quantity. She hands over everything, including her many, many sins. Love, because it is a sharing and a need to recognize the other, removes all the walls of separation.

The Adulterous Woman (Jn. 8: 2–11)

According to the Pharisees, judgment comes from the Law which condemns and leaves one to himself. According to Jesus, judgment stems from the heart that recognizes and reunites. The Pharisees leave, one after the other, heavy with a sin they have not recognized, because they expect to receive justification from themselves alone. The woman leaves justified, because she has presented to the Lord nothing but her misery, being incapable of the slightest good on her own. In his sovereign independence, Jesus, who knows the secret of hearts, writes on the ground with his finger.

The Good Thief (Lk. 23: 39–43)

He, too, recognizes Jesus, while the one who insults Jesus thinks only of himself and of vengeance. For us, it is justice. But for him! Remember. The prayer of the sinner is perfect. It is like David's: I have sinned against God. What can Jesus do in the presence of a person who gives himself in this way? He has come to show the mercy of the Father to defenceless people – the poor, the children, the sinners. This evening you shall be with me in Paradise. Go out into roads and invite to the wedding everyone you can find (Mt. 22:9).

4. Some Scriptural Prayers for Sinners

A psalm that recapitulates the action undertaken by God on behalf of his people: Isaiah 63 to 64. You do not cease being our father and our potter even when we have saddened your Holy Spirit. You turn away your face and let the deadliness of sin develop within us. But you return; you do not abandon us for ever to the power of our crimes.

Then there are the so-called penitential psalms, in particular Psalm 130(129): "Out of the depths . . ."; and the great psalm of the sinner, Psalm 51(50): "Have pity on me in your goodness." Of both of them we could say: we can never recall our own sin without mentioning Israel, the whole people that God reconciles along with us. The individual's perspective and that of all men are bound together. As for the second psalm, the great *Miserere*: in praying it we verify the fact that man never comes to really know himself without simultaneously being given a greater knowledge of God. In the admission of sin, I come to know God upon whom I rely. I come to know him as mercy, him who looks upon me with tenderness and pity. I experience his justice, because I no longer have any justice; and it is he whom I ask to teach me the depths of justice. I rely, moreover, upon his unique holiness, so that I may be washed and become whiter than snow. It is especially his love that I experience in this divine transformation which follows the admission of sin – that love through which I receive the joy of a person re-created in the presence of the Holy Spirit. Finally, transformed by this love, I can communicate to others the experience I have had: I will teach sinners your ways. I know, moreover, that, if my words have any effect, their efficacy comes from grace: Lord, open my lips. Thus, whoever we are, in a crushed spirit that no longer has any hope other than the blood of Jesus, we can offer sacrifice, the only sacrifice that pleases God.

This prayer unfolds in faith and in grace: In the midst of my sins, "exercise your Goodness and your Mercy, and You will be known in them" (St. John of the Cross). We can make our own the admission of the paralytic of Bethzatha (Jn. 5): "Lord, I have no one." That means: in the variety and yet universality of evil in which I am immersed, waiting together with so many others for a healing which never happens (the paralytic has been there for 38 years), I can only cry out to God from the depths, as in Psalm 18(17). This is the cry that makes God come down. "Rise up and walk." It is the creative word which resurrects the dead, just as the Father has shared this power with the Son. "I have no one"; that is, "I have only You."

5. *The Triple Colloquy* (Exercises *63–4*)

After we have dwelt some time on the points that have struck us most in the preceding meditations, St. Igantius supposes that we will prolong our prayer by addressing, in turn, Our Lady, the Son, and the Father. Each time, we ask them for a triple grace: to go to the heart of sin, that is, not to the material act, but to that which comes from the heart of man and makes him impure (Mk. 7); to feel the disorder of my activity, that is, that double heart which wants to serve two masters (Lk. 16:13) and that dim eye that plunges the whole body into darkness (Lk. 11:33–6); and finally to know the world, that world which means being wrapped up in oneself, that world in which the love of the Father cannot exist (1 Jn. 2:15–17).

6. *Mercy and Judgment (Hosea 1 to 3; 11; Matthew 25:31–46)*

Her who was the unfaithful wife I will marry for ever "in justice and in righteousness, in tenderness and in love". By means of chastisement, I will bring her to life again: I am God and not man.

Clearly, love pulls the winning trick. "We are judged on the basis of love," says John of the Cross, thus summing up the great judgment scene. Those who share in glory are those who were found within the movement of the Spirit of love, even if they did not yet recognize him towards whom this movement was leading them – Christ in each one and everyone. Each person is judged on the "reality of the law inscribed in his heart" (Rm. 2:14–16), the reality of the Law that is love.

It is possible to have not recognized Christ and yet to be one of his sheep, one of those who has not sinned against the Spirit (Mt. 12:31–2). Others have correctly identified him but, nevertheless, are not admitted. It is not those who say, "We have prophesied in your name" (Mt. 7:21–3). The Lord does not enclose men in any category, social or religious; his own come to him from all over (Mt. 8:11–12).

Thus, even if your conscience brings no accusation against you, do not judge yourself or others. Just let the Lord come (1 Cor. 4:3-5).

PERSEVERANCE IN THIS PRAYER, REPETITION, EXAMEN

This prayer does not become personal unless it continues. The Russian pilgrim repeats it over a long period of time, and his heart is transformed by it. At this point in the retreat, St. Ignatius suggests the repetitions, where each individual returns to those points where he has "felt a greater consolation or desolation or a greater spiritual sentiment" (Ex. 62) – in other words, on those points that did not leave him indifferent. The preparation for prayer, therefore, consists not in doing a lot of reading or in pre-planning a dissertation, but (to the extent that our spiritual experience has developed) in freely focusing our attention on those points which we know from experience will help us easily discover God.

To facilitate this repetition, St. Ignatius suggests the triple colloquy, which we have mentioned above.[1] In ordinary life, everything can nourish this prayer: reading Scripture, the liturgy, the examination of conscience, penance, the sacraments. . . . Through these means, an attitude is formed in us which earlier generations called "compunction", that "crushed" heart which God never despises. It is a unique sentiment that, like every work of the Spirit, reconciles apparently contrary dispositions: confusion, shame, wonder, thanksgiving. It keeps the heart malleable and always open. It is the source of action and of radiance. It contributes to the maintenance in our life of justice and purity of motivations. It is a state of permanent conversion to love.

In this connection, we should say a word about the examination of conscience. We have already remarked that it was a grateful recognition of God's gifts.[2] It is also, as we shall point out later,[3] a manifestation of our secret thoughts in the frequent

[1] p. 60
[2] p. 30
[3] pp. 182-183

remembrance of the Lord Jesus. It helps situate me in the truth of my being, where the Father judges in secret and where, following the counsel of St. Augustine, I tell him what I am. *Dic Deo quod es.*

This examination has its place during the retreat just as during my ordinary life. The best way to make it is a "manner of praying" according to the examples given by St. Ignatius in the *Exercises* (238–48). Thus I learn to receive from God the knowledge of myself that he wants to give me. I learn to encounter Jesus Christ there in the very depths of my being, in the "inside" where that which dirties a man originates (Mk. 7:21).

THE SACRAMENT OF PENANCE

The prayer of the preceding days prepares us for this sacrament and finds its fulfilment there. Having descended into the depths, we give Jesus what we are and he gives us what he is. The sharing of baptism is renewed in the sacrament of penance. We no longer belong to ourselves but to him.

One of the causes for the current disaffection with the sacrament of penance is perhaps that we have regarded it primarily from a psychological and moral point of view; we sought merely greater self-knowledge and moral progress. We must go beyond this concern for purification and good conscience. That which forgives sin is love, sin's contrary.

Living in Christ, I live in love. My desires, my thoughts, my actions take place in him: "It is no longer I who live; it is Christ who lives in me." In my growth in him, my very sin (and if someone claims to be without sin, he makes a liar out of Jesus [1 Jn. 1:10]) no longer belongs to me, as soon as I recognize it as sin. It is absorbed by him who is "the propitiatory victim for our sins – and not only for ours, but for those of the whole world" (1 Jn. 2:22). He, like the act that condemns me, is nailed to the cross (Eph. 2 and Col. 2). Even if I were as covered with faults as the sinner-woman at Simon's banquet, my sins are forgiven because I have "shown much love". Simon, who remains just in his own eyes and who judges others, does not receive pardon, because he has "shown little love" (Lk. 7:47–8).

Just as two persons who love one another yet live far apart experience the need to manifest in signs (and not merely by the spirit which unites them) the love which is in them, so also the Christian who lives in the love of Christ experiences the need to express in signs his continual reference to Jesus Christ.

The sign of our reference to Jesus in the very midst of our sin is the sacrament of penance. Just as in the Eucharist, I participate in the sacrament of penance, not as in some magic rite or in an anxious manner, but out of love's need to express in a perceptible way my twofold recourse, to Jesus Christ and to the community of my brethren. I am wrapped in sin; the recourse to the sacrament is the acceptance of salvation in the way Jesus gives it to me. Just like the admission of my sin, it signifies my acquiescence in the Lord's repossession of everything that makes up my life, including the evil.

It is from this basis that I can answer those questions which often I incorrectly ask first. When should I go to confession? How should *I* go to confession? The forms – the sacramental discipline – can vary over the centuries. The important thing is to rediscover in these forms the depth of my relation to the Lord. We should not let the sources of life be corrupted.

AT THE END OF THESE TWO DAYS: DISCERNMENT

There are two ways of approaching discernment which are not opposites but which are located on different levels. For many people, discernment is an exercise of judgment that applies to the things in which we are involved or to the feelings which we experience a certain number of criteria for determining what pleases God and what does not. Tradition, however, beginning with St. John and St. Paul, understands discernment rather as the exercise of a sense – a "touch", a "flair" – which is part of the make-up of a baptized person and which develops to the extent that charity grows.

The first kind of discernment is a critique. It is that of the psychologist or of the theologian. It presupposes study and competence. It distinguishes the respective domains of nature and grace. It re-examines the data of tradition, in order to deepen and adapt them in accordance with the perspectives of modern science. In particular, with the Gospel and St. Paul, it assumes as a principle that the action of God can be detected only after the fact, in the light of its effects, in the light of the fruits of the Spirit, as St. Paul says. Thus, in the meditation on sin, the only contrition that it recognizes as coming from the Spirit is a contrition that opens the heart to more love. This kind of discernment is situated within the logic of a faith for which God is a God of love, whose will gives meaning to life.

The discernment we are going to speak of is of another order. It does not entail a rejection of the critical sense or of psychological scrutiny, but it is situated beyond that, in a sensitivity to the movement of the Spirit. If forced to use a comparison to understand its nature, we would refer to what happens in the artist, the man of action, or the lover, when they are in the presence of the object of their activity. They do not disdain reason, science, or the data of tradition; but, when it comes to acting, they obey other norms. They are like a man who does not have to ponder in deciding upon a colour or a sound. His habitual way of exercising his senses makes him decide spontaneously.

This discernment which is the exercise of a sense presupposes that we are not outside the reality we are judging. We can enjoy music without making music; but, if we want to sing, we must first make sure that our voice is on pitch. Thus it is with someone who, in a spiritual experience, wants to know if what he feels is true or false. He cannot make this judgment as though it concerned some reality exterior to himself. First of all he must test himself and, even if he should happen to be a great expert in this matter, rediscover himself as a small child. He is entering into an adventure where what he has learned in books is not very useful for him at first. Unless his language and his study have been rooted consistently in his experience, he does not recognize at first what he is experiencing, even though he has seen it described in his studies. This is the case with a person's first experience of love. What is genuine, what is false? What sort of life have I entered into? These are questions that Ignatius asked himself at the beginning of his conversion.

Obviously, for the sense of discernment to be exercised in this way, the first condition is that we enter into a world where we risk losing our habitual points of reference, a world we have no control of, even though it does not force itself upon our freedom. How could a person for whom God is not an object of search or desire but of mere curiosity enter into this discernment? He would have to speak from experience, and yet the world of the Spirit is not a reality for him. For various reasons, he has even learned to disdain anything that does not fall within the domain of reason or that eludes empirical verification. He has not heard the call to Abraham, to leave his land with no proof other than the word that is given to him.

The beginnings of such a procedure awaken a good deal of resistance. Each of us experiences this when he agrees to give himself with a bit of seriousness to the adventure of a retreat. All sorts of objections present themselves. "It's stupid!" "It's pure feelings!" "I'll never last." "Brainwashing!" "Other people don't do this." "What will they think of me?" "I am cutting myself off from everyday life." "This kind of experience is a luxury that most men cannot allow themselves." We could continue the list of similar reactions. In the final analysis, each person is alone before the unknown. Perhaps after the first moments of enthusiasm have passed, we no longer have anything before us except the dismal desert or sunken roads without horizons.

These resistances are fundamentally nothing but defences raised up against a call to leave oneself. When God appears in his truth to manifest the secret of hearts, man will go hide himself like Adam in Paradise. He does not like to feel naked. It is only with great difficulty that he allows himself to be opened up and his secret thoughts to be revealed.

What should a person do in the face of these resistances, which St. Ignatius in his vocabulary calls "desolations"? One should not change anything that he has previously decided. You are in the night; do not set out in a new direction. Hang on and be patient "with firmness and constancy". If you want to change something, be aware that the problem lies within you. Pray more; do penance, obviously on condition that these means do not render your efforts even more difficult. They are only means; so you must use them with flexibility towards the

goal of "finding what you want". If they bring about the opposite result, it is because you are treating them as absolutes, not
to find God but yourself. In this case, it would be better for you
to relax, sleep, or chop wood. Basically, you are trying to extri-
cate yourself on your own, in an area where mere reflection and
mere effort are not enough. St. Ignatius, shaken to his very
depths by temptation to suicide, cries to the Lord: even if I
have to follow a puppy, I will follow him, provided I find you,
Lord. The Psalmists and Job cried out to God in the same
way.

A great purification is accomplished in this struggle. It
makes a person pass beyond false fears and childish joys. Like
the agony of Christ, it moves in the direction of life, of love, of
peace. It is especially faith that is deepened here.

There comes a moment when we sense that something has
changed. A certain joy, a certain cheerfulness takes hold of us.
These feelings can be located at various levels, all the way from
the superficial enthusiasm of the person prepared for every
sacrifice to the quiet peace of the person for whom God has
become everything. In any case, a breeze has passed which dis-
persed the preceding night. I am no longer the plaything of my
sadness or of my reasoning. Something happens, something
like what takes place between two lovers who rediscover one
another after a long series of difficulties: the winter is past, the
rains are over. In general, it is only afterwards that we notice
the change. While it is happening, we are caught up in the
wonder of it all. But going back down the mountain, our heart
is no longer the same. "A burden has fallen from our shoulders."
It is the time of consolation, says St. Ignatius. There we
recognize God from the life, the joy, the strength that he
inspires.

Is that the end of the matter? To think that would be an
illusion, as we learn at our own expense. There is a temptation
to appropriate the gifts of God for ourselves. Each one hoards
the riches of his experience. Once again, everything is com-
promised. After the consolation, there is the night again, the
search, the desert. Everything seems thrown back into question.
All the creative people, all the men of action, all those who
really love – they all know these painful hours. Those who seek
God know them just like the others. They learn then that the

75

gift given to them is pure gratuity: "The Spirit blows where it will." And it withdraws if you try to clutch it in your hand.

At such times, the person becomes insensitive again and does not know what to think of his condition. Just a while ago he saw; now he sees no longer. As a matter of fact, his insensitivity would be dangerous if it indicated more the inability to get outside himself than the inability to seek God. But this insensitivity is often merely apparent, if the person, reduced by it to his powerlessness, experiences the increasing desire to open himself and to love, if his infantile fears disappear (for they have merely the appearance of contrition), and especially if his gaze is fixed more firmly upon our Lord who saves him.

Then we receive something different from, and greater than, what we had expected: not some emotional thrill but a conversion in faith, a feeling of solidity and peacefulness that gradually takes hold of a person in the depths of his being. "I have never meditated on sin with such peace." Yet a little while ago, the one who said this at the end of these meditations would have found this peace abnormal. Thus we begin to leave that subjectivism in which the religious life is often enclosed, especially in the beginning, without thereby falling into an intellectualistic dryness. The feelings, once awakened, are nevertheless transcended in order to receive from God something other than what they usually crave. The struggle for discernment removes the ambiguity that hovers above the word "feeling", not through an analysis of it as an external object but through the experience that it brings about.

This adventure is never finished. What we have just discussed holds true for all periods of life. Thus, with increased confidence, each person should remain humble and vigilant. His strength comes from somewhere else. He must always remember this, under the danger of compromising the progress he has already made.

In short, one of two things is true:
– Either I am in peace. If so, I remain active and vigilant, so that I do not fall asleep there. The second state would be worse than the first (Lk. 11:24–6).
– Or I am in distress. If so, I work to shake off the fear and to rediscover my strength in Christ. Man of little faith, why did you doubt? (Mt. 14:31).

In any case, consoled or not, I must force myself at each moment to get out of myself in order to let Christ grow. It is in him that I find my balance, but I can maintain this balance only if I continue walking. And this "ever-growing charity overflows into that refined touch that allows a person to discern the better . . . for the day of Christ" (Phil. 1:9–10).

SECOND STAGE:
From Conversion to Mission

In the depths into which the preceding days have made us descend, Jesus has risen a bit higher on the horizon of our life. From him, we can hear the call to mission: just as my Father sent me into the world, so also I sent these men into the world, that they be one like you and me, that the world may believe that you have sent me. Conversion of the heart and call to mission – two stages which reveal the work of the Son. He does not descend into the depths except to lead us into the heights, in order to fulfil all things (Eph. 4:8–10).

These two stages are continuous and inseparable. Christ frees us only to win us over. No one can say: "Lord Jesus, have pity on me, a sinner", without immediately hearing: "Come, follow me; I will make you a fisher of men" (Lk. 5:1–11). Conversely, no one takes part in the work of Christ unless he has first recognized himself as a sinner. The prayer of the sinner and the prayer of dedication are but one and the same prayer.

The coming days make us enter more intimately into the reconstruction of mankind by Christ, to make of mankind a "new creation", his Spouse, that which it is in the plan of the Father.

In this all-embracing work, each of us has his particular mission. I must listen, in this call addressed to all men, for what is addressed to me alone. Within the global election, there is the particular choice.

In meditating upon the call of Christ and in contemplating the mysteries of his life, I will discover the way in which I can best correspond to this plan. Prayer becomes a slow preparation for the election, the personal acceptance of God's plan for me.

IV.   The Call of Jesus

The coming days are not an aimless stroll through the mysteries of the life of Christ. We are given a unifying thread to follow: the meditation on the Reign, the call.

Everyone more or less knows how this meditation is presented in the *Exercises*: "the call of the temporal King . . . in order to contemplate the life of the eternal King" (*Ex.* 91). The parable of the King seems obsolete. Perhaps, like the parables of the Gospel, it has a hidden meaning: the call of Christ comes to us through the call of man.

At any rate, this meditation is merely a point of departure. Each person catches an imperfect glimpse of the reality of the call, and must then set off from where he finds himself. Thus he readies himself to hear still better. Understanding and life are inseparable. The understanding of a vocation develops as it becomes action and life.

We speak so ambiguously about vocation, dedication, apostolate, service of others, and the gift of oneself, that it is good to make a few remarks before beginning the meditation:

1. The call is addressed to everyone. In one sense, we can say: every man has a vocation which he must discover if he is to make a unity of his life. In particular, each Christian who is converted to Christ hears his call to be re-created in his image and to work for his Kingdom until his definitive coming.

2. A vocation is more a person than a job. This is true on the human level: a man discovers the meaning of his life the day he discovers the love that constitutes the centre of his life. It is the same with Christ. Many people refer to Christ or claim to serve him, even though they are merely practising an ethic or defending a cause. To the extent that Jesus has failed to become a living person, the works undertaken on his behalf, however generous

they might be, risk foundering in the bitterness of failure or the success of complacent adulthood. That is why, before saying "I want to do this or that", it is important to ask myself, "What does he mean to me?"

3. A vocation is always out ahead of us. Many people, in order to be faithful to their vocation, want to return to the time of its discovery. A vocation is not a treasure to be protected against loss, but a life to be developed. Like the knowledge of persons, it is a continual discovery, without our ever being able to exhaust our understanding of it. We have never finished entering into our vocation.

Hence the attitude I try to assume: rather than worry about whether or not I have a vocation (thus making this question an object of study or analysis), I force myself to assume a position where I can hear the call of the one who gives my life its meaning; and, once I have heard it, I advance from the point I am at. I pray that "I may not be deaf to the call of Our Lord, but prompt and diligent in accomplishing his holy will" (*Ex.* 91).

THE CALL OF JESUS

Whoever hears him is called simultaneously in two directions: in the horizontal direction (because he is universal, and everything is recapitulated in him) and in the vertical direction (because he is exclusive, and everything is directed towards him alone). In the same way, the response given to this call is simultaneously an acceptance of everything and a transcendence of everything.

1. *The Call of Man*

This is already the call of Christ, because Christ contains everything that belongs to man and to the earth. In our desire to serve the Reign, we risk forgetting this aspect. How many Christian or spiritual lives remain crippled or impoverished through ignorance, fear, or contempt of the human! Even in sin, man retains the imprint of God, whose image he is. In order to hear the call of the Lord, and to work with him, a person must first consent to hear the call of the man that he is – and which all those who form the universe are. Before thinking about dedicating himself, a person should think about being himself.

We could show how, throughout Scripture, God's action manifests this profound respect for man and this determination to make him attain what he is. A few examples will suffice: David in Jewish history; the pagans in human history; the apostles in the Gospel; the sense for culture and humanism in the Church (though not without groping and awkwardness). Under the watchful eye of God, in each and every age, under an immense variety of conditions, mankind "begins again its terrifying task". Man must first of all be human.

But what is this "human" that must be promoted?

There is in us the danger of arrest. In our desire to promote man, we create false gods for ourselves; we dehumanize man by abandoning him to his desires, to false progress, to an enslaving technology. Man no longer knows who he is.

Throughout his research, his achievements, his conquests, man becomes himself only if he opens himself to the forces of love in freedom and mutual respect. Love is the moving force of our history, and we become ourselves only through love's personalizing dynamism. It is the sense of love that we must find first of all if we are to live the rest. This is the first call that we must hear.

The parable of the temporal King's call should bring us to this realization. Man, in order to respond to God, must discover in himself the sources of commitment, of devotion, of love, of the greatest service. In this promotion of man through love, there is the beginning of a consecration and of a renunciation. Man will be himself only if he discovers the depths of all the responses of love: gift, service, radical self-sacrifice.

The call of Christ, who calls man to something further beyond, is part of this movement. It is the movement of the creative Word who incarnates himself in order to lead all mankind to God. To respond to this call of man is, therefore, already a response to the call of Christ: whoever is not against me is with me, says Jesus in Luke 9:49–50.

But the Lord also says: whoever is not for me is against me

(Mt. 12:30). This saying announces the counterpoint, the call of Christ in his exclusivity. Everything is to be brought together, but together with him.

2. *The Call of Christ*

Christ, the incarnate Word, both attains and shatters all limits. He leads from the fullness of man to the fullness of God. His call concerns all mankind, but it can be addressed only to the individual, in his most intimate depths, in that freedom which allows him to open up to the call of love and to the greatest service. This is the source of the double, personal-universal character of that call.

This call is an invitation to realize in each of us what was realized in him. He came from the Father to return to the Father, having gathered up with himself all mankind. St. Peter, after Pentecost, presents the work of Christ as that of the last times. These last times, first realized in him, must be extended to the whole of humanity (Acts 2). As Paul says in Ephesians 4, he descended into the depths in order to lead everything back into the heights. He accomplished this work through his cross, having lived all things in love, even to the point of death itself. This is the greatest service: to give one's life for one's loved ones.

What he accomplishes in himself through his cross and resurrection, in suffering and in glory, he continues to accomplish in those who believe in him. It is for this purpose that he chooses men "who are with him" and gathers together communities of disciples after the Ascension. The Church is the mystery of his universal love which is realized in each particular community, where he is present simultaneously to each individual and to all collectively. The movement of the life of the Lord continues in each individual man and in all men; it makes all of us go with him into suffering, in order to be with him in glory.

In him everything is recaptured beyond what we can imagine or construct. All persons and events become revelations of God and find their sole consistency in the unique event of Christ's Cross and Resurrection. That is why Christ calls all men to follow him with his cross through everything, so that everything may be transfigured. Everything happens in the personal

84

universe of the Christ of glory, as mankind in him becomes a concrete reality, in the image of the Trinity of persons.

This reality is expressed in various ways by the various evangelists. The synoptics say it one way, St. John in another, St. Paul in still a third way. But for all of them, it is the same reality that is revealed under its double aspect of intimacy (he with me, the life of the Trinity) and universality (fullness, the all).

The danger is that we stop prematurely or try to seize things by force. This is the permanent temptation of all forms of messianism and of all churches. The Kingdom becomes a human construction, closed in upon itself, the service rendered to an ideology. Once Christ is got rid of, conformed to our desires, or reduced to human size, then those who make use of his name lose the very meaning of man which they claim to promote. Love dries up within them.

The Kingdom is exclusive. Christ alone fully satisfies the universal aspiration. Each person must pass through him to reach the goal. He is exclusive, so that he might become everything.

3. *The Response of Man*

This response is given in a seemingly contradictory twofold attitude, one of acceptance and transcendence.

It is first of all a matter of "obvious good judgment and reason" (*Ex.* 96) that a person would give meaning to his life by consecrating his entire self to this work, like those workers for the Gospel who do not content themselves with mere talk. This work refers not only to explicitly apostolic tasks but to all human endeavours. Every human task has its place in the Kingdom, since it is the expression of the will of the Father, without which we could relegate it to the profane or secular. In reality, like the soldiers who consult John the Baptist, we are invited to work wherever we find ourselves. The Lord has consecrated in himself the entire human order, taking up into his Body and into the Eucharist "all the work of men".

But we are invited to "more", to use the expression of the *Exercises*. In order "to distinguish ourselves in total service" to

85

the universal Lord, it is not a question of choosing this or that particular role, as if one were more important than another, but rather of attacking within ourselves the way we accomplish it, whatever be the object of our choice. The manner of the Lord is that of the "servant" who loved to the very end. It is the "way of love", the way of Christ who has loved us and given himself up for us (Eph. 5:2). It leads us along with him to attack all self-seeking and self-love in ourselves. It does not ask us to limit nature, as though it were evil, but to let nature grow only that we might dedicate it and surpass it. This is the most radical sacrifice of the "Come and follow me". I discover this more and more to the extent that I consent to live as a full human being without holding back anything for myself, in the exclusive gift of my humanity to the person of Christ. All that is best in man is taken up to be burned and transformed on the cross. I must be baptized with a baptism of fire.... I have come to light fire.

We would not expect this kind of conclusion to our medita-tion on the Kingdom. Nevertheless, there is no other way of responding integrally to his call. I receive myself in order to give myself. Man achieves his fullness only by living in Jesus that movement which is at the heart of the Trinity, where none of the divine persons is himself except in giving himself to the others.

4. Hence, "An Offering of the Highest Value" (Ex. 98)

This offering takes its origin in my most intimate depths, where the Father sees in secret, where I am alone before him. I freely choose to desire him alone – not that I might do this or that, not to gain a reputation among those around me, but to be with him alone, in the midst of the greatest contradictions and contempt. Whatever happens, I will be happy. It is you alone that I desire. I accept you for better or for worse.

But in these depths where I am alone with him, I suddenly rediscover myself in the company of the whole universe. Called by him and with his help, I make this offering with Mary, with the saints, and with that "cloud of witnesses" who believed in the word of God and, along with Abraham, set off without knowing where they were going (Hebrews 11).

86

In this offering, I rediscover the whole Reign of Christ in both of its correlative characteristics, universal and exclusive. Having lost everything for him, I receive everything in him. Whoever loses his life for my sake finds it (Mt. 16:25).

The contemplation of the Reign, as it is presented above, can serve as the prayer for this day. It might be good to take one aspect or other, according to the various Scripture texts.

1. *How Jesus Presents Himself (Lk. 4:16–30)*

This passage describes the reaction of Jesus's first hearers when he outlines his programme in a speech in the synagogue of Nazareth – a contradictory reaction of amazement and rage.

In him God manifests his Kingdom, his universal gratuity and mercy, as Isaiah had announced (Isaiah 61). His fellow citizens admire his words, proud of being his compatriots: he is "from among us". Yet he refuses to let himself be enclosed within any category at all: Eliah was sent to the widow of Sarepta, a foreigner, and Elisha to Naaman the Syrian, a foreigner. People will come from the East and the West to take part in the feast of Abraham (Mt. 8:5–13).

Jesus disconcerts us at the very moment that he seduces us. He stirs up our desires and then draws us beyond them. This behaviour led him to the death of the cross. And that implies that we should follow his example (Lk. 9:23–7 and the references indicated in this section).

2. *The Description of His Reign: The Book of Consolation (Isaiah 40 to 50)*

In all of Scripture, this is perhaps the most marvellous picture of the Reign of God realized in Jesus Christ. The whole work of

God, from beginning to end, is presented there, the first events and the last, the old covenant and the new, the former and the new Exodus, with all its prolongations. We can read this book without ever exhausting it.

Especially the Servant-songs:

42:1–9   The signs of the Spirit in him whom God has chosen to be the light of the nations.

49   In you whom I have called, I will glorify myself unto the ends of the earth. Through you, I will accomplish the wonders of the return.

50   In the midst of outrages, I entrusted myself to him who gave me the tongue of a disciple. Happy are those who hear my voice.

52:13 to 53   Here the event is recounted still one more time: the arm of God is revealed in the humiliated servant, to whom God has entrusted the multitudes.

"Today this is accomplished in me" (Lk. 4:21).

"Such is the work of the Lord" (Ps. 22[21]:32).

3. *Its Manifestation in the Infirmity of the Flesh: "The Word Made Flesh" (Jn. 1 to 2:12)*

Everything is said in the Prologue (1:1–18).

The Word made flesh, or the fulfilment of the unthinkable ("There is no union possible between God and man." Plato, *The Symposium*), so that we might come to know the Unknowable and become sons of God.

He is manifested by John the Baptist (1:19–34).

Faced with the immense expectations of man ("Are you the one who is to come?"), he answers, but not as we expected. He is in our midst. The Spirit of God is upon him. But he presents himself as the Lamb of God, that Lamb predicted by Isaiah, the perfect Servant (Isaiah 53). It is in the weakness of the flesh that he comes to save, the Wisdom and Strength of God (1 Cor. 1:17–25).

John the Baptist, the friend of the Groom, waiting attentively and lovingly for him who is coming (Jn. 3:27–30), shows in his own person how to receive and recognize him – by the intensity of desire. The little ones and the poor are not disconcerted by the humility of the Kingdom: "I thank you, Father, for having revealed this to the very little people" (Lk. 10:21–2). "He has come in great pomp . . ., for the eyes of the heart which see wisdom" (Pascal).

He is revealed to a few disciples (1:35–51).

He calls each of them by his own name: "You search me and you know me. You have laid your hand on me" (Ps. 139[138]). No one call is like another. Come and see, he says to the first two. And Jesus looked at Peter. Follow me, he said to Philip. Here is a genuine Israelite, he says of Nathanial. I saw you under the fig tree.

Yet, from the very beginning, all are united by the same faith in him: Rabbi, you are the Son of God. However, they are told that they have seen just the beginning of his wonders: You will see heaven open. To follow Christ means to accept never being beyond the beginning of discovery.

The call to "pass beyond" towards the hour. Cana (2:1–11)

The Lord does not refuse signs, especially if they manifest the goodness of the creator: do everything he tells you, says Mary. And Jesus performs the miracle. But Mary must understand that he has come for another wedding feast, his "hour", where Mary will be present and where he will give on the cross the wine of the new covenant in his blood. No one will be able to break up that marriage.

In order to be admitted to the Kingdom, I agree together with Mary, to "pass beyond", to be admitted at the time fixed by God. With her, I hold myself ready for what "I have not yet heard" and for "what has not occurred to my heart".

This long meditation on the Incarnate Word permits us to hear the burning words of John in the prologue of his epistle: "what was from the beginning . . . that we announce to you . . . so that your joy may reach its fullness" (1 Jn. 1:1–4).

4. The Work of the Lord: Master, Where Do You Live? (Jn. 1:38)

This question of the Baptist's disciples can be taken as the subject of my prayer. Beginning here, I can ask the Lord my questions about himself and his work. Scripture and the Gospel will nourish his responses.

Lord, who are you?

In silence, I will hear him spell out all of his names, all those that Scripture and the Liturgy give him: Word, Light, Life, Image of the Father, First-Born of all creation, the One, Spouse of humanity, the Victorious One. . . . With all these names, the Church has multiplied hymns in his honour.

The essential point is that I understand that he is just as alive for me as he was for the apostles: Christ yesterday, today, and for all ages.

Lord, what do you want to do?

He will say to me: I have come to re-do what was undone, to renew the obscured Image of the Father at the heart of humanity, to find the lost sheep, to reunite the scattered children of God. All of this begins with the community of disciples (Acts 2:42–6). I can re-read John 17, Eph.1, Col. 1.

How do you want to do it?

He will say to me: I did not come to satisfy you with a reassuring but superficial triumph. I came to re-establish things in the truth.

I am the sole and true Priest, who dissolves in himself all covenants and who, sent by the Father among men, opens up for himself, through his death, the path of love and of life, so that he can draw all men along with him (Heb. 1 to 10:9). In him, the cross is victorious.

What do you want of me?

"By wondering if you will do this or that future thing well, you are not so much testing yourself as you are testing me; for if it comes to pass, it is I who will do it in you" (Pascal, *The Mystery of Jesus*). Yet I can do nothing without you, if you do not open your heart through faith. Take your place among the cloud of witnesses who have preferred "the opprobrium of Christ to the riches of Egypt" (Heb. 11 to 12:4). Give yourself as they did, and in their company.

5. *The Offering: Are You Able to Drink My Chalice?*
   (Mt. 20:20–33)

How can I assure myself that this offering is genuine?

Spontaneously, I am speaking like the mother of the sons of Zebedee (According to Mk 10:35–40, it is the sons who make the request. Mother and sons have the same spirit.): "On your right, on your left. . . ." This mother is conscious of the gift she has made of herself and of her sons. Jesus does not scold her, but purifies her request.

He demands that a person offer to drink his chalice, that of the will of the Father, who gives salvation to all men without distinction, and who, in order to bring about this salvation, offers his Son the condition of a slave, or servant (Phil. 2). This is the chalice of absolute giving and unselfishness. You shall not behave like those who exercise authority (Lk. 22:24-7). I am in your midst as one who serves. Among you, it makes no sense to speak of first and last.

"We can do it," respond the apostles. Do they understand what they are saying? Undoubtedly not. It is enough for them to know that it is his chalice and that they will drink it with him. It is he whom they desire, not some particular form of service. Love leads to this kind of response.

If we are afraid in making this offering, it is because we are thinking more about ourselves than about him. Let us ask for an open-hearted love: "I make my offering," says St. Ignatius, "with your grace."

No doubt there are many other texts that could be suggested. Moreover, the Reign of the Lord takes more than just one day to sink in. It is little by little that we enter it; now this text, now that text will help us as the years go by. "This is how you should think; but if you think differently on some point, the Lord will enlighten you" (Phil. 3:15). St. Paul, in trying to make the faithful understand the Reign, learned to take time seriously.

DISCERNMENT AT THE END OF THE DAY

This contemplation adds several landmarks along the road of discernment, by harmonizing us with the spirit of Jesus. In this matter, many people discover what a difficult thing this discernment is.

First of all, a certain number of illusions collapse. Placed before the conditions for a genuine gift, we discover those things that frequently contain false, ambiguous, or unreal elements – our grand declarations about the service of God, of man, or of the Kingdom. Moreover, this meditation, begun with a certain enthusiasm, can end up in resentment or dryness. With this meditation begins a task of scouring and scraping.

Our reactions to the prayer of this day also clarify the degree to which our relationship to Our Lord has been personalized. Once I am invited to pass on to the level of mystery, of life, and of relationship, I experience with sadness how much my pretended religious life remains a mere abstraction. For many different reasons, my self remains closed in upon itself: a lack of affectivity, an inadequately developed personality, restricting my goals to the realm of ideas or of a task to be completed. I think I am seeking the Lord, and I discover only myself. I must break away. What is proposed to me is the struggle against "sensible and earthly love", to use the expressions of St. Ignatius. We did not expect that the call to the Kingdom would end with this invitation.

This necessity of struggle, in turn, clarifies another point: how much the world of grace remains unreal to me. Something is supposed to take place in us that does not depend upon us alone. Now, frequently in the service of the Kingdom, we stay on the level of virtue, of personal effort, of duty. We ask: what are we going to do? How should we do it? We must dismiss, back to back, the attitudes of both the cocksure person who wants to work everything out for himself and of the timid person who considers himself incapable or who broods about his own weakness and sins. In both cases, I am thinking more about the programme to be accomplished than about the Lord who helps me live it. The Kingdom, as a divine reality, develops itself in each and every person in a divine manner, that is, according to the grace bestowed by the Spirit. As for this greatest service that I aspire to, I ask to be admitted to it through grace.

Little by little, the depths of this offering become clear. The Lord does not wait until we are perfect to be with us. He is not waiting for our accomplishments but for our gift of a heart that offers itself as it is this very day. The kind of humility which says that it has everything to gain proves its authenticity by rejecting all forms of fear.

V. Mary, or The Perfect Response

THE PURPOSE OF THE DAY: THE MYSTERIES AND THE MYSTERY OF MARY

In the spirit of the meditation of the Reign, we begin to contemplate the mysteries of the life of Christ, in order to impregnate ourselves with his spirit and thus to recognize his will. The ideal would be to have a lot of time to let this impregnation take place. One of the benefits of the *Exercises* made over a period of thirty days is that they permit this extended contemplation. Through the very act of contemplating, I become one in spirit with the one I contemplate.

Today, in Mary, I hear the perfect response, the *fiat* of the creature to her Creator. It is the response of her who never ceases to receive herself from God, whose freedom knows neither yeses nor noes. In her, humanity rediscovers what it is. Also in her, the Trinity sees its work accomplished. That is why Mary is the perfect example for every spiritual life, for the response to every vocation, for the human being who allows himself to be transformed by the Spirit. In her, the tension between freedom and grace finds its perfection.

In contemplating the mystery of Mary, we come to understand our own mystery and the way in which we are being transformed by the work of the Spirit. Prayer refines and simplifies itself. It becomes acceptance, openness, relaxation, intimacy. The refinement that occurs is simultaneously the condition and the effect of this contemplation.

CONTEMPLATION

This word is one of the most commonly used words in religious literature; and, like many terms in this same vocabulary, it is open to many ambiguities.

It could not be a question here of a reconstruction of the past, of pious flights of imagination, or of moral applications that take off from the Gospel stories. Through these stories, taken as means and signs, we seek to enter into the living, here-and-now presence of the Lord, in order to receive the grace and light of "Christ who lives in our hearts through faith".

Of course, in this connection, we can speak of method. St. Ignatius invites us, in turn, to "see the persons", to "watch, observe, contemplate what they say", to "watch and consider what they do" (*Ex.* 114–16). But the important thing is to grasp the meaning of the suggestions that Ignatius gives. Their purpose is to help us pass through the visible to the invisible reality, to help us feel the "silent depths" (Paul Evdokimov) of the events presented in the Gospel.

Thus there are in contemplation, as in each event lived by the Word made flesh, two elements:

– The one is the perceptible, the element of representation. This element, like the flesh of Christ, is indispensible in our movement towards God. But it must be put in its proper place. We should fear both dwelling too long upon it and also neglecting it. The Jews, when faced with it, remained at the perceptible level and demanded miracles; the Greeks despised the flesh and were scandalized by the Incarnation. Both remain outsiders to the mystery of the incarnate Word. Even today we oscillate between these two extremes.

– The other is the invisible. The temporal event, upon which the historians and exegetes concentrate, retains the value of sign. I am not so attached to it that I cannot discern in it the Son of God. As in the liturgy, I latch on more to the mystery than to the event. Certainly, today I cannot be content with the naive way in which the old authors made these contemplations; they let themselves go, it seems to me, in unrestrained trips of fancy. But these old authors, to the extent they were making an authentic contemplation, were not duped by the proposed method. Their authentic prayer took place in faith and in the application of what they called the spiritual senses. One detail was enough to focus their attention. From there they moved to an attitude of adoration, of wonder, of respect, of receptiveness, of desire. This is how they encountered Christ. I try to live the event as it was lived by the apostles, by the first Christians who read the accounts of it: faith made them present to the risen Christ, still living within them.

Thus, what I am seeking is the knowledge of Jesus Christ. This knowledge shows itself in my prayer through the following two characteristics:

First, it discovers in each event the divine and universal dimension. It is a reading of the fact in its interiority and depth. Thus, in contemplating the Annunciation, I go back to the Trinity's decreeing the salvation of the human race; for my gaze embraces the universe with "all the men on the face of the earth". Looking at the Nativity, my gaze penetrates to the cross itself. Thus, I focus more on the meaning of the event within the unique mystery of Christ than on a detail that is mentioned or on the way the story is told to me.

I am seeking especially the "intimate knowledge" of the Lord. Not that kind of knowledge which leaves the object known exterior to the knower and which, as exact as it may be, cannot bring me to the reality of the thing but merely lets me use it. For, we do not come to know a person by using him; we would be merely possessing or dominating him, while the person himself would elude our grasp.

There can be no personal knowledge unless the one aspiring to know the other holds himself defenceless before the other: "Leave everything", "Take off your shoes", "Follow me" – various formulas that express this first necessary phase in knowing another. It is to the extent that I agree to descend to the depths of my being that I am able to encounter the depths of the person I want to know. But here it is God who is giving himself through Christ, and God is inexhaustible. I have committed myself to a road whose end constantly escapes me. The marvel is that, between this "I" which empties itself of itself and this God, an encounter does take place. For we are called to let Christ live within us. This knowledge in the Spirit is something completely different from an external imitation. Christ unites himself to us and continues himself in us. And yet all of this is nothing but a beginning.

Really, this knowledge of Jesus Christ is an adventure of love. The human experience of love can give us some idea of this discovery of Jesus to which we are called.

But I do not see this Jesus Christ, while I do see the person who opens himself to my love. This is true only at first glance. Certainly, the quest of love begins with the visible. That is why I begin to get some hint of God precisely in the love I receive from others and which I give to them. However, in human love as in the love of Jesus Christ, I quickly enter a world beyond the senses. I must discover, beyond what the other registers about himself in the visible world, that which does not fall within the realm of sense. Every real interpersonal relationship is an entrance into a world where sense and analysis have no mastery. It is the world of the freedom and originality of each person. There it is that I come to know the other in an indescribable embrace.

It is at this level of being, that of love in a growing freedom, that I must place myself in order to catch some glimpse of that "intimate knowledge of the Lord" that I request, "so that I might love him more and follow him" (*Ex.* 104).

This knowledge is, therefore, an experience of the whole person when he is awakened by the Spirit to the reality of love, by means of these mysteries. Whoever contents himself with sentiments or displays is stopping short, just like the person who makes his love of another into a matter of fleeting emotions. Life never ceases to make us enter more intimately into the reality of the one we love. Life assimilates us to the other through the heart's effort at resemblance. Thus it is with the knowledge of Jesus Christ: it develops in faith. It produces in us the resemblance which transforms us through the action of the Father and the Holy Spirit. No one comes to me unless the Father draws him. You are a letter of the Holy Spirit. The "prodigious presence" of the Word-made-flesh (the liturgy of December 30) thus becomes more real than even the mutual presence of persons in our perceptible world. There we enter into the heart of the Lord, in order to share his attitudes and to make ourselves perfectly one with him. It is in this resemblance that we know him.

In this domain, there is no substitute for experience. Suggestions are helpful; they help us to follow a more direct path and not to stray into illusions. But there comes a time when each individual must enter into hiddenness. The experience of love cannot happen through some intermediary person. Come and see (Jn. 1:39). "Now we have heard him; we no longer believe because of what you have said" (Jn. 4:42).

1. *The Annunciation (Lk. 1:26–38)*

This story, read and re-read by so many generations, places us, as does the story of the creation of man, at the heart of the mystery of God and his encounter with humanity. By means of the exegesis which has been done on this story, the one praying tries to attain the reality beneath the words and spiritual attitude of Mary. He can only beg insistently for that intimate knowledge of the Incarnate Word which Mary had, so that he may thereby discover his own vocation and how to respond to it. Before a mystery of this kind, there is the danger that we will seek mere ideas rather than seeking to grasp the inexhaustible taste of the mystery.

Beyond the words of the angel, it is God's plan for humanity that is unveiled: let us make man in our image and likeness. "Reflecting the glory of the Lord as though in a mirror, we are transformed into that image" (2 Cor. 3:18). "He has made us know the mystery of his will . . .: in the fullness of time, to gather all things together under one sole head, the Christ" (Eph. 1:9–10). With Mary, covered with God's gifts, humanity begins to understand what it is: the Lord is with you.

Humanity also begins to know him through whom it becomes what it is: You will give birth to a son . . . and he will be called the Son of the Most High. The Word-made-flesh set up his dwelling among us, and through him "grace and truth have come to us" (Jn. 1:17). Man grasps the last word about himself only in discovering the one whose imprint he bears.

This flesh, through which he becomes our life and unites us to the Father (Jn. 6:52–8), is the work of the Spirit in Mary: "The Holy Spirit will come upon you", the Spirit through whom all things are created and who makes us enter into the intimacy of God. He is in Mary, to form the life-giving flesh of Jesus. He is in us, to transform us into his resemblance.

The Annunciation begins the new age:

"The earth will be filled with the knowledge of God." The Three Persons are presented here as "bringing about", as Ignatius says, "the redemption of the human race" (*Ex.* 102). All men are involved in this plan: "see all the men on the face of the earth" (*Ex.* 106). Mary, like Eve, appears here as the mother of the living.

This blood-relationship established between God and man through the flesh of Christ is the work of freedom. For he is born "not of a desire of the flesh nor of a desire of man, but begotten of God" (Jn. 1:13). Mary turns towards God, to give her consent to the work of the Spirit. She conceives her son first in her heart, before begetting him in her body. This is how Tradition has spoken about this event, thus showing that the birth of the sons of God takes place only with the consent of man. Who is my mother and who are my brothers? He who does the will of my Father in heaven (Mt. 12:46–50). You become the son of the one you have decided to resemble. Mary, who turns the desire of her heart towards God, becomes his mother. That is why the announcement made to Mary about the marvels to happen in her takes the form of a call and an invitation.

Mary becomes the model for the response of the creature to the love of the creator. Eve diverted her attention to herself; she lost herself in discussions about the divine command; she put distance between God and herself. Mary does not know these deviations. She remains true before God: she sees herself, but in truth, as a work of his love. A perfect mirror, who opens herself to the light, to let it reflect in her and who lives in the recognition of God's gifts. We call her "Immaculate", for she has resisted the efforts of Satan to make us turn our eyes in upon ourselves and turn them away from God.

Even the promise of the fruit of her womb does not impress her with her own importance. She does not jump at this promise, in the avid manner of Eve. She first tries to determine the origin of the Spirit who is speaking to her. It is only after recognizing the source of this Spirit that she voices her astonishing words: I am the servant of the Lord. Let it be done to me according to your word. In the same measure that she hesitated just a moment before, she now gives herself. No protests of false modesty, no fear. Nothing is impossible for God. Elizabeth, the sterile one, has become fruitful. God can make her, the virgin, his mother. She is nothing but a servant.

Thus Mary plants her feet in faith. She has no other light than the one she has just received: "You are blessed, you who have believed . . ." (Lk. 1:45). She will not stop growing in this fundamental attitude, which will lead her upright to the foot of the cross. While she waits, Mary does not stay fixated upon God's gifts. As soon as "the angel leaves her", she "leaves for the mountainous country". For her, giving to others springs spontaneously from the encounter with God.

The entire mystery of a vocation – every human life is henceforth a vocation – is lived in the mystery of the Annunciation. "How will this happen?" From the time of Abraham (Hebrews 11), God's call leads man towards the impossible, the unbelievable. There is no ground under his feet. There is no road marked out. We no longer find the habitual securities. To advance, we, like Mary, have nothing but faith, together with its consequences (including the cross), its obscurities, its solitude. This is the risk of love. Mary has made her commitment.

Is it on purpose that St. Ignatius, usually so reserved in his presentations, expands to such an extent upon the contemplation of the Incarnation? At any rate, this mystery demands to be repeated in all its divine and universal dimensions. That is why, in order to nourish the prayer of this day, we may not want to take up any more mysteries. Everyone should follow the lead of the grace that moves him.

2. The Mysteries of Mary

In the light of the Annunciation, each one can let the sequence of the mysteries of Mary unfold, through the cross up to the Resurrection, the Church, the Assumption. There we discover the itinerary that God makes a person follow, once he has communicated his life to him.

Mary is the one who, in coming to know the God who gave himself to her, never ceases to move on and seek further. Like the psalmist, she says: "Reveal your movements to me." Or again, like the spouse of the Canticle (2:16–3:5): Return! The beloved has given himself to her, but she can keep him only by continually seeking him. During the night, alone, I looked for him; I ran through the streets and the public squares, and I did not find him. I asked the city guards. It is only in going beyond all these things that, finally, I met him whom my heart loves. The mystics, like St. John of the Cross, used these images to describe this continual "passing beyond", this continual struggling upwards. This applies to Mary, to each of us, to the Church.

In this struggle upwards, freedom opens itself up and grows. It receives from God only that it might open itself up to a new demand and let God manifest his marvels within it. Freedom enters into the realm of the Spirit: "Those who are animated by the Spirit of God are the sons of God" (Rm. 8:14).

3. *Nazareth and the Loss of Jesus in the Temple*

Two mysteries which, by way of contrast, express two aspects of each vocation and each life in Christ.

Nazareth

It is everyday, human, natural life – the first place God is to be sought. There is no gleam of mystery shining through here. We are at the heart of the humiliation of the Son of God, beneath the weight of the scandal expressed by Job and by many of the psalms: how long will you leave us in this state? It is in this everyday world that the Virgin silently discovers the face of the Christ, the Word-made-flesh, that is described in Philippians 2.

This life is the life of the Church in the midst of humanity – not as it is manifested through the apostles (the "official" representatives), but as it exists from day to day in the believers. It *is* – period. The Spirit lives in it, in this hidden condition. Something eludes us, something that makes us different, yet without any of it being revealed. It is the condition that is described in Hebrews 11, in the sense that we have received existence and live in faith.

This everyday life is not dull, because it is lived in the presence of the Father and in the Holy Spirit. Something happens there under the influence of the Word which is "like a lamp shining in a dark place, until the day begins to break" (2 Peter 1:19). It is the time of waiting. It is a march in the night under the light of faith. It is a daily presence to that which is. See. This Law "is not beyond your means nor beyond your attainment. It is extremely near you; it is in your mouth and in your heart, so that you can put it into practice" (Dt. 30:11–14).

The Loss in the Temple

This is an event that causes rupture and questioning, a flash of lightning in a serene sky. Why, if this was the will of the Father, didn't Jesus tell his parents in advance? Neither Mary nor Joseph would have opposed God. But God, who demands that we love our parents, also demands that we leave them, so that we might recover them again from him on a new level, that of universal love. It is to this "passing beyond" that Jesus invites Mary and Joseph. Once it is accomplished, everything falls back into silence. But the heart retains its imprint.

This event is the symbol of what happens in Mary, from the Annunciation, the Purification (here it is the question of the "sword of sorrows"), all the way to the cross. The Virgin lets herself be drawn along by this everyday life that continues to repeat itself. She lets the word of God penetrate her heart – this word of God which, like a sword cutting through to the very marrow, initiates her into the mystery of the Hour and makes her glimpse in the cross of her Son the victory of God.

At first she does not understand the word. But she maintains her heart in attentiveness and desire. She holds herself in the attitude of Wisdom. And, after having meditated upon these things for a long time within her heart, she stands upright at the foot of the cross, not surprised by the event.

The entire story of Mary is contained in these two episodes, which gain their symbolic value from what happens in our lives and in the life of the Church: the march in faith, through realities that are at times banal and at times unexpected. The cross is always present, not to hinder our march but to give it meaning.

4. *The Mystery of Virginity*

Virginity is the climate in which Mary lives the mystery that is hers. Not ignorance or fear of the condition of man and woman. What if that had been the tenor of her marriage with Joseph! No, rather according to the saying of Christ (Mt. 19: 10–11), a free decision of her heart on behalf of the Kingdom of heaven.

Virginity as lived by Mary is the sign of the fulfilment of the Kingdom. It is as though, in her, the love that is at the heart of each person tended, not only to personalize itself to the highest extent, but also to universalize itself. In Christ Jesus, says St. Paul, there is no longer male or female, Jew or Greek, slave or freeman (Col. 3:11 and Gal. 3:28). That means: in Christ, there is no longer any subjection among men; now there are only free persons who freely decide to love. Humanity, both man and woman, has arrived at its full maturity. At the same time, humanity has gone beyond this age "where the children of this world marry and are given in marriage". The love of God, which makes them his children and delivers them from death, makes transparent in them a love which, bestowed upon each person in his individuality, nevertheless shows no exclusivity. God through Christ has become everything in all men (Lk. 20:27–40). Virginity is no longer mere celibacy; it is the choice of a heart that responds to the gift of God and which has a new way of loving. It is that towards which all forms of love are tending.

To be precise, virginity in Mary is not the exclusion of marriage. It corresponds, rather, to the invitation of St. Paul (1 Cor. 7) to persevere in the state where we discover our call and to use this world (whether it is a question of the relationship between man and woman or of diverse social conditions) as though we were not using it. "The time is short." "The shape of this world is passing away." "The Lord is near." That is why the example of Mary, even if it applies above all to those called to be "eunuches for the Kingdom" (a divine folly), applies to each Christian who lives out a form of human love. All true love tends to "virginize" itself (Teilhard). The important thing in this domain, more than the carnal reality, is the attitude of the heart that tends towards God and lets all of its love develop in him. "The only really chaste soul is the one that gazes at God without interruption" (St. Basil).

This love, which finds its beginning and its term in God, is the love that the Church wants to live in its various earthly circumstances: Husbands, love your wives as Christ has loved the Church (Eph. 5:21-5). All the loves known here below rise up to this love as to their summit. That is why the virginity of Mary, the new way of loving the humanity realized in Christ, pertains to the very mystery of the Church.

REFINEMENT AND SIMPLIFICATION OF PRAYER

Inside the experience under way, there takes place, in one way or another, a deepening of prayer. The meditation of the previous days was the work of the intelligence which receives something, thoroughly chews and tastes it, and then extracts a morsel of wisdom. The contemplation proposed here supposes a new degree of interiorization. For Wisdom incarnated itself, and its Incarnation makes this contemplation possible. This contemplation is a presence to persons, a transformation of the heart, a mutual sharing. Through it, the being of Christ passes into me, his Spirit is given to me; and, through his actions, I come to know the will of the Father.

To permit this deepening, each person should discover his own way of praying, the way in which the Spirit bestows himself upon him. Why try to contemplate all the mysteries? A few are enough: St. Ignatius proposes only two a day. Afterwards, each individual should return to one or the other – whatever helps him most.

The various suggestions given above can help us simplify our prayer even more, without thereby making us the prey of imprecision and fantasy. It would be good to reconsider the remarks on the different methods of prayer (*Ex.* 238–60), in particular the suggestions on posture and breathing. They will help us understand how to keep our attention fixed on the mystery by means of a vocal prayer. This is the sole purpose of the rosary. It does not really matter how you say it. The repetition is not tedious except for those who do not know the riches of the prayer of the heart.

We also get some idea of the exercise that Ignatius calls the "application of the senses". It is directed to those spiritual senses through which, if God wills, we have just come to taste the "infinite gentleness and sweetness of the divinity, of the soul and its virtues, and of all the rest, according to the person we are contemplating" (*Ex.* 124).

The heart purifies itself immensely in this simplification. It forgets itself and proves the saying of Cassian: "Prayer is not perfect if the person is conscious of himself and realizes that he is praying." It is only after the fact that he who has been seized realizes that something has happened, something vital, which he often finds hard to describe. Nevertheless, if he has to speak to others, this experience communicates a new warmth to his words, without his suspecting it.

Little by little, we discover the simplicity in prayer that is possible to the Virgin, who finds God in everything. This is the prayer of true contemplation, which is enjoyed by all those who, cloistered or not, have no other desire than to be faithful to the Spirit.

This prayer tends towards the objectivity of faith. For it confronts us with a given, the mysteries of Christ in time. At the same time, it accepts the fact that revelation is imparted to us in the unfolding of our personal time, according to the stages and circumstances through which this discovery leads us.

This prayer does not enclose itself within the impressions we have felt or in the ideas that spring up. It is careful not to make itself the measure of the Gospel nor to interpret it in one's own way. There is a certain nakedness of the text, a certain distrust of feelings or applications, a certain sobriety, all of which favour the discovery of the essential. The conformity of what I feel with the Tradition of the Church and the understanding of exegesis both help to maintain me in the objectivity necessary for prayer.

Nevertheless, we penetrate the object of our faith through means other than reason, study, or reflection left to themselves. It is the light of the Spirit – the unction that John speaks of (1 Jn. 2) – that lets us enter and taste things from the inside.

Moreover, concerning the effort expended, we must find a balance between a nervous attention to the object that leads to fatigue and a lazy relaxation that leads to illusion. As St. Ignatius says, the matter for discernment is more delicate here, *"subtilior"* (*Ex.* 9). We must experiment in one direction, then in another, in such a way that, through these trials, God helps us feel what is right for us. In short, this prayer which at first seems simpler requires, as do all simple things, a greater discernment.

In this search, a profound purification takes place in our feelings as well as in our intellect. We cannot satisfy ourselves with pious appearances or theoretical constructions. This prayer of the marvelling gaze requires profoundly humble persons, persons stripped of themselves and full of peace. It is not astonishing, therefore, that we feel rising up within us all sorts of resistance, sadness, and shock. It is a new world that is opening up for us, this way in which the Lord and the Virgin view existence. We have everything to learn, and the habitual points of reference are not of much use.

But from this total experience, our intelligence acquires a

new delicacy, that "refined touch" that allows us to discern the better, that sense or taste that allows us to "feel and taste things in the interior of the heart". "You have the anointing; the only thing necessary now is that someone instruct you." The roads leading to this knowledge are frequently austere, but they lead to a greater discernment. What good things those people deprive themselves of who are called by the Spirit but fear to undertake the adventure! What goods they deprive the Church of!

VI.   Discernment: The Manner of Christ

THE PURPOSE OF THE DAY: THE WISDOM OF CHRIST

We are arriving at the summit of the *Exercises*, because we are at the point where all objective discernment takes place. Here we try to harmonize ourselves with the manner of God, which we then want to apply to the choices in our life. This manner is the fundamental attitude of Jesus, who manifests the Father's love in all his actions.

At the heart of the spiritual experience, we stand before this law: faced with any choice, in whatever state I find myself in – single, married, or religious life – what makes me a disciple of Jesus and makes me perfect like the heavenly Father is perfect is the fidelity to the invitation of the Lord to be poor, to become a child again, not to belong to myself. No one comes to the Father and no one can love his brothers unless he follows Jesus along this road.

In each particular decision, we are invited to return to the source of all perfection and freedom, from which we can emerge into love. From this point of view, we distinguish Christian virtue from all the others, as beautiful and generous as they may be. In each vocation, in each task, in each apostolate, we cannot claim to be spiritual adults or genuinely committed if we do not try to maintain this mentality of the poor man. We run into intransigence on this point – the intransigence of Christ in the Gospel. This intransigence constitutes the fundamental structure of the human freedom that readies itself for grace, because it guarantees our harmony with the will of God.

In the face of this ideal, prayer becomes more intense and attentive. Who could understand this wisdom unless he were admitted to it by the Spirit of God? To prevent his being over-awed by anything and to counteract the merely apparent aspect of things, St. Ignatius proposes the great meditation of the

Two Standards; and at the end he invites the retreatant to address the Virgin, Christ, the Father, asking "to be accepted". No one arrives at this summit unless he is led there. That is why, in addition to meditating, we must pray.

The Struggle to Be Undertaken

The meditation "of the Two Standards" is a meditation of light; it places us at a lookout-point from which we see the world, mankind, and history with the view of faith formed by the Scriptures. Two camps, two cities, two loves are tearing at the heart of each individual as well as at the heart of humanity as a whole. Whoever acts according to the truth and opens himself to love must decide to join the struggle imposed by this view.

This meditation is an explication of the meditation of the Reign. It clarifies the commitment already made. That is why the grace requested is first of all a grace of light, that of discerning the real good beneath appearances: "The knowledge of the true life" taught by Christ, and "the grace to imitate him" (*Ex.* 139).

The imagery, or set of symbols, employed by St. Ignatius, since it follows the example of Scripture, often leaves the modern mind uncomfortable. The personalization of evil, of sin, and of temptation under diabolical forms and powers is an obstacle for modern man. Without going into these discussions (which are far from being settled), let us concentrate on two points which are sufficient to ensure our ability to pray: whatever our way of understanding Scripture's affirmations about Satan and the spirits, we must clearly recognize in ourselves both the occurrence of temptation and the necessity of a struggle if we are not to succumb to it; secondly, rather than fixing our attention upon the evil and the danger, we should instead focus upon the positive reality, that of Christ who chooses and calls us. Many people delay on the questions raised about the existence and sin of the first Adam, though they would do better to consider the existence of the second, in whom grace has superabounded (Rm. 5). Neither Scripture nor this meditation warrants a pessimistic view of mankind, arbitrarily

divided into good people and bad people, with the subsequent
danger that we place ourselves among the good, judging the bad.

1. *The Universal Temptation*

It begins with the will of a person who possesses something
and becomes fixated upon his possession – whether it be the
esteem of other men, immediate success, or power in any of its
forms. The person ties himself to a good which he makes into
"his" good: body, money, success, undertaking, perfection.
Having made himself the centre, he identifies himself with the
thing he desires and makes it into an "in-itself", an "absolute"
which he adamantly desires, to the point of crushing whatever
prevents him from achieving his ends.

Thus, an obstruction is produced. Intelligence and freedom,
no longer having any rules beyond themselves, turn in upon
themselves as though within a closed world. Man, having
become an absolute, having no more points of reference, is
incapable of finding within himself the answer to the eternal
questions; he remains inexorably alone. He creates for himself
a world where love for the other becomes impossible. Trapped
within himself, incapable of seeing and loving the other, he is
like the rich man in the Gospel who, evening after evening, fails
to see Lazarus standing right in front of his gate.

This temptation touches all of us. We make everything – our
virtues, our undertakings, and the rest – into our exclusive
right. We could describe this immense seduction as it expresses
itself everywhere – in our groups, in the world, in the Church.
It begins with the good that each one bears within himself or
with the ideal that a person fashions for himself. Since it has to
do with real goods, this temptation wins us over all the more
easily if we pay no attention to its mechanism. The more we
advance, the more subtle it becomes, this temptation under the
appearance of the good, this temptation of the Pharisees, of the
perfect person, of the person who sees clearly and who credits
himself with great feats of service. *Corruptio optimi pessima*: "The
wicked angel transforms himself into an angel of light and at
first goes the way of the faithful soul, so that he can ultimately
lead the soul his way" (*Ex.* 332). This is the state that spiritual

writers formerly called tepidity. It is not apathy or weakness; the image, which makes one think of tepid water, is not a good one. Rather, it is a condition of self-satisfaction in a state that was good, but which becomes the occasion of our ceasing to advance. Each person is plagued by this, for the very reason that he is right or because he has done well. The good becomes an accomplishment, a possession, a cause of strife. Some Christian communities become the image of a world where division reigns; and yet at the start, each individual desired the good. It is an immense deception.

The temptation that must be overcome constantly is that of using our power or wealth for our own purposes, in order to build a world for ourselves; and each person is rich and powerful in some way, spiritually or otherwise. Whatever form it may take, "my little children, do not love the world" (1 Jn. 2).

2. *The Invitation of Christ*

Christ, clothed again in power and wealth, never ceases to receive them from the Father and to direct them towards the Father. His centre is outside himself. That is why he is the perfect Image of the Father. He is the perfect Servant who justifies the multitudes (Is. 53). He is never alone; the Father is always with him. For every man, he is the Way. In him, each effort and each search reaches its goal. Poor, he is always free to love.

Here we find ourselves at the heart of the apostolic preaching: "The Lord of the whole world chooses all these men – apostles, disciples, etc. – and sends them throughout the whole world to spread his sacred doctrine among men of every state and condition" (*Ex.* 145). The universal temptation is fundamentally nothing but the negative counterpart of that universal call. It is precisely because all men should become sons of the same Father and because this transfiguration of their being can be accomplished only in freedom that they experience within themselves the resistance and call of the self that refuses to give itself.

So that the impossible commandment to "love your neighbour as yourself" can be realized, the heart of man must open itself to a love that does not come from itself. For the love at stake here is a participation in the life of God, not merely a virtue to be practised. It presupposes a faith in him who communicates love in its intimate depths and its universality.

Now, it is only the heart of the poor man and of the infant that can be invaded by love. Jesus alone was this poor man and this infant. In order to make us participate in his nature, he invites us to become poor men and infants along with him. That is why "he recommends for his servants and his friends to try to help all men by drawing them first to poverty . . ." (*Ex.* 146). So that men might love one another, the Lord invites them, whatever their conditions or circumstances, to form with him a Church of the poor. He thus sets straight the orientation of the heart of all men. Instead of riches, instead of a self that creates its own worth and asserts itself, exercise poverty; and, along with me, do not fear either humiliations or contempt. With me, come to know humility; then the love of the Father will manifest itself through you. Learn from me that I am meek and humble of heart.

Whoever re-reads all of Scripture from this point of view suddenly realizes that it is the focal point that clarifies everything. The entire teaching of Moses, the Prophets, the wisdom books, and especially Jesus strives to remove from man's heart the seduction of appearances and of false salvations. We are well within the bounds of any spirituality, at the source of all perfection. Only the person who ceaselessly abandons himself can live and grow in love. Thus, we are invited to a great battle, that of freedom. In this battle, as long as we are on this earth, there are no limits and no periods of rest. It is nothing but the following of Christ. All the Saints, even if they expressed it differently, were saying the same thing: there is no peace or freedom with Christ except in a greater self-renunciation.

PRAYING TO BE ACCEPTED

Even less in this meditation than in that on the Reign, it could never be a question of my effort. My understanding, enlightened by faith, glimpses the truth; but it is not a purely intellectual consideration that makes me achieve the summit I have glimpsed. Only prayer can open up my freedom to love and make me desire to be poor with Christ poor. That is why I am invited to address Our Lady, Christ, and the Father, asking to be seized by the movement of love which, having begun in Christ, continued in the Virgin and the saints: "I ask to be received."

The request for this grace reminds us of the episode in the life of St. Ignatius known as the vision of *La Storta*. On his way to Rome with his companions, Ignatius there sees the Father assign him to the Son who is carrying his cross: "I want you to take him with you," says the Father. It is the transformation of the two into one, the perfect resemblance of hearts in the union of wills. St. John of the Cross designates this state as the mystical marriage. Different expressions of the same reality. The summits simultaneously of perfection, of love, of union, of divinization. We are at the heart of the divine work that wants to unite all men in the Son. It is the perfect union, which we always tend to locate anywhere but where it really takes place.

It is not surprising that we feel overwhelmed. We are at the heart of the vocation of the man called to become God. At this point, the question is whether this "over-man" should come about through a power that he wants to attribute to himself alone or rather through the recognition of a power that comes to him from somewhere else. We are in the presence of the Two Standards or the two manners of becoming what God has made us: Satan or Christ.

The cross looms on the horizon; for through the cross of Jesus Christ God has successfully transformed our world into a personal universe, a universe of love. The universe of Satan – the "world" in the sense of the Gospel – is closed and hardened, because it has shrivelled up upon itself and its possessions. It is a universe of solitude and fear. Christ gives the poor heart the freedom to give everything, even its own life, in order to save love. Because of this choice, Christ dies; but through it he rises, eternally living and free.

We are asking the Spirit of Jesus to develop in us a wisdom that will help us to live as Jesus lived. The reading and re-reading of Scripture throughout our life develops this wisdom. It teaches us how to distinguish real instances of salvation from the false and how not to be seduced by appearances. The text proposed here are meant merely as examples.

1. *Solomon's Prayer for Wisdom (Wisdom 8:17 to 9)*

It is the prayer for requesting Wisdom.

It is already an instance of discernment when a person recognizes in the gifts of nature the gifts of the Lord. It is all the more so when, in order to accomplish our destiny in our fragile bodies, we seek the source of all wisdom in the Spirit of God.

Cf. Sirach 51:13–20. The search for wisdom.

2. *The Criterion for Judgment: The Beatitudes (Mt. 5:1–12; Lk. 6:20–6)*

The granting of happiness to the poor is the sign that the salvation of God is among us. No one is saved through his own merits. You who have no money, come (Is. 55:1–6). The poor have nothing to boast of. In calling them, God manifests the gratuity of his love. They are invited to the wedding feast – people who were gathered up off the highways, who had never anticipated such a feast (Lk. 14:12–24). Or again, they are like the defenceless infants whom the apostles send away, yet who are the very ones to whom the Kingdom belongs (Lk. 18:15–17 and other corresponding texts). Better still, they are like the labourers of the eleventh hour or the undeserving sinners who then have precedence over the sons of the Kingdom (Mt. 9: 9–13; Mt. 20:1–16). In all these poor people, God makes his universal mercy burst into the light.

Those to whom Wisdom has revealed its secrets try to fashion for themselves the heart of a poor man. For the gate is narrow (Lk. 13:22-4). The only ones who enter by this gate are those who, once they are called, preserve throughout their life a sense of the gratuity of God's gifts and who do not consider themselves better than other men just because God has chosen them. Who are you to think that you are better than your fellow-worker? (Mt. 18:23-35). The only attitude that will keep your heart open to universal love is the one perfectly exemplified by the attitude of the poor man in need. St. Matthew, in his eight beatitudes, describes this one attitude under its various aspects.

Unhappy the man, on the other hand, who, having achieved some degree of perfection, develops the attitude of a rich man. He encloses himself within his gifts and becomes incapable of letting love enter into his life. The rich man wants nothing to do with the misery of Lazarus; quite simply, he does not see it, preoccupied as he is with himself and his own welfare. Wealth, every form of wealth (that is, every good thing from God which is possessed for its own sake) shuts the eyes and hardens the heart. This is the case with the Pharisee who considers himself better than others and fails to respect the mite of the widow (Lk. 16, the whole of which concerns money and the Pharisees, the friends of money; Lk. 21:1-4).

The poverty to which Jesus invites us is not primarily an ascetical poverty, like that of the philosopher or of Diogenes in his tomb; rather, it is the attitude of a heart that is free in the very midst of its possessions and ready to love the other, knowing that it has received everything and has a right to nothing.

Faced with this ideal, the prayer of the sinner becomes: *Out of this sinner's heart fashion for me a poor man's heart, and I will receive your love.*

3. The Magnificat (Lk. 1:46-55)

The prayer of the Magnificat is a view of the world and of humanity in the light of the Beatitudes. A résumé of the prayer of the Old Testament, it has become the canticle of the Church. We should sing it, to beg for and learn discernment.

The Virgin Mary makes God the principle of her thoughts, and she understands herself only in him; he has looked upon the nothingness of his servant. She has also discovered joy. What men search for so strenuously, this little daughter of Israel has found at the very outset. This is how God deals with those who recognize his mercy.

Adhering to God with her whole heart, Mary goes beyond appearances and does not let herself be scandalized by the prosperity of the wicked (Ps. 73[72]). Like the psalmist who reflected on this for a long time, she entered into the mystery: God sends the rich away with empty hands and remembers his love.

Along with Mary, the Church – each one of us – witnesses to the fidelity of God, who remembers his love to the extent that we accept our poverty.

4. *The Law of the Community of Jesus's Disciples (Phil. 2)*

The success that Jesus expects from us is the success of love. Hence, the many invitations of Paul to "make his joy perfect" by having but one "same love" among us. This is the success sought by those who have the same attitude that Christ Jesus had. This kind of success makes us similar to the perfection of God-love: "Be perfect as your heavenly Father is perfect" (Mt. 4:43–8).

The way to succeed in this is to imitate the manner of Jesus. Because he was of a divine condition, he did not cling jealously to the dignity he had a right to. The humiliation of the Word, the incognito of God (Ratzinger), are ways in which God makes himself known as love and spreads love. He does not pretend to be man; he becomes man. He does not say that he loves; he becomes what he claims to be. And that leads him to the cross. In everything, he submits himself to love, which for him is "worth more than life" (Ps. 63[62]:4).

That is why the Father glorifies him in his humanity and manifests himself in this humanity. Cf. 1 Cor. 13:47. If you want to know whether the love in you is divine, examine its effects: eager to serve, not envious, . . .

Again, James 3:13–18. Two kinds of wisdom could be leading you. You can tell if the kind leading you is divine – and not earthly, purely human, or even demonic – by the fact that it makes you act in meekness, with peace, tolerance, and understanding.

5. *The Struggle: The Temptation of Christ in the Desert (Lk. 4:1–13)*

This scene is the model for the struggle to which Christ commits us, in order to continue in us his victory over the spirit of hate and division, the prince of this world.

Jesus, still glistening with the water of baptism and full of the strength of the Spirit, encounters "all the forms of temptation" as they actually occur in reality, originating in some real good: bread, or the right to exist; wealth, or the right to possess; success through seduction, or the will to use things for one's own ends. Satan turns a means into an end, in which he then tries to imprison us. Each time, Jesus breaks the circle. Each time, he moves on to the Father: the Word, the nourishment of man; the adoration that is due to God alone; the obedience which, in order to believe, needs no miracle. If a sign must be given, it is the sign of Jonas (Mt. 12:38–42), of that man who, sent to preach of mercy though he was in total despair, entrusted his cause to God and was delivered by God. It is the sign of the cross, the sign of faith and of universal love.

This temptation heralds the decisive battle, that of the agony, where Jesus meets once more these two orders: his will for an immediate victory (Isn't his cause the most just?) and the will of the Father, who, in the midst of evil and hatred, shows the face of love and "conquers evil with good" (Rm. 12:21).

When St. Paul invites the Christian to arm himself, he is thinking about this battle: not against enemies of flesh, but against the spirits of evil (Eph. 6:10–20). To wage this battle, we must "pray at all times in the Spirit".

6. *In the Midst of Obstacles and Persecutions (Lk. 21 : 8–19)*

The counsel of the Lord is: Watch out that no one trick you (Mt. 24:4). Do not let yourselves be deceived by either seducers or persecutors. Difficulties will assail you from all sides – from those who profess to be men of God, from your friends, from your relatives. Put your confidence in the wisdom that will be given to you. Not a hair of your head will be lost. Your strength is in your constancy.

Those who put their confidence in the name of Jesus, even "those without learning or culture" (Acts 4:13), surprise people with the force of their replies and come to know "the joy of suffering insults for the name" (Acts 5:41).

This confidence, which is the wisdom of the fools of Christ (1 Cor. 1 to 4), constitutes the essential element of the demand made upon the disciples of Christ. It opens for them the secrets of freedom, of joy, and of the knowledge of the Father (Lk. 9:57–10:24).

7. *The Depths of the Struggle (Jn. 7–12)*

To illustrate the depths of the struggle (to which the disciple of Jesus is committed, in order to recognize true salvation), we could re-read John 7 to 12, chapters in which the opposition increases between the Pharisees, the sons of the devil, and Jesus, the son of God. It is the drama of the religious man who either opens or hardens his heart to the coming of the light, who either recognizes or rejects God in Jesus.

The world (which each person discovers in himself to the extent that he shuts himself up among the gifts of God, in order to claim them as his own) is the place of this intimate and universal struggle (1 Jn. 2:12–17).

THE RULE FOR OUR CHOICES: THE TWO CRITERIA (*Ex.* 333)

The rule given here is merely the personal application of the meditation on the objective discernment proposed to us by the Two Standards. We examine not only the object of our desires ("Is it good?") but also the way we desire it ("Is it conformed to the manner of Christ?"). Without our even noticing it, everything can be fouled up by the way we desire things.

That leads us to ask the following question: even when I possess or desire something that is conformed to the moral law, to justice, to the Gospel, or to the teaching of the Church, do I possess or desire it with freedom of heart, purely and solely for God? I cannot consider an ideal to be the will of God for me just because I have glimpsed its beauty or because someone has proposed it to me. The excellence of the object can be deceiving, as in the case of all those ideals that arose successively in the Christian consciousness – the kingdom, evangelization, development, etc. I must come to desire this object without self-seeking, in peace, and with confidence in grace alone. Thus, by stripping myself of my self, I receive as a gift from God the perfection I desire.

Two criteria should play their respective roles: that concerning the matter and that concerning the manner. On the one hand, I offer myself without reticence to what I see as the better. I am bothered even if I merely slip from desiring the better into desiring something less good. The repugnance I experience at first does not indicate a non-call; I try to conquer this repugnance by praying and offering myself. Yet on the other hand, if after long and sincere prayer and especially after a long passage of time, I am still not able to embrace this object with peace, it is a clear sign that I am the one constructing this ideal or that, at least for the moment, I cannot make it my own. I thereby learn that the better-in-itself is not necessarily the better-for-me.

We would save ourselves a lot of difficulties and would be more efficient in action if we would apply this rule at the beginning of our reflections about our choices and vocations. We would discover at its very source that "carnal love", as the spiritual authors used to call it, which we unknowingly hold on to even in those desires and acts of devotedness of ours that seem the most unselfish.

This way of getting down to the heart of our motivations relativizes everything; that is, it helps us to consider them not as negligible, dangerous, or secondary (in themselves, they are neutral) but rather in their relationship to the essential. Poverty is not primarily the absence or privation of things, but the shedding of self so that we can become interiorly free of things, whether we keep them or get rid of them. It is in this interiority, with all my understanding and all my possibilities, that I seek to bind myself to God and thus to abandon myself.

VII.   Education for Discernment, Election

THE PURPOSE OF THE DAY: THE MANNER OF CHOOSING

I ask the Lord to be taken, to be received. I offer myself along with Peter: I want to follow you in life and in death. I will give my life for you. Wherever you lead me, I will follow you.

Peter spoke these words and was mistaken. The generosity of his heart and the grandeur of his plan did not shelter him from such mistakes.

Under which conditions can I permit myself to speak these words? How can I guarantee that, in a choice that seems good to me, I am being faithful to the plan of God? This question raises simultaneously the questions about education for discernment and about the election that this education permits. A certain disposition of heart, maintained and developed throughout our life, guarantees, at any given time, the conformity of our choice to the Spirit of the Lord.

THE ELECTION: WHAT IS IT ALL ABOUT?

This word comes from the Ignatian vocabulary and demands an explanation.

There is a danger that we will understand the election as an act through which a man who is sure of his motivations and who has weighed the pros and cons finally decides upon one alternative. This act of freedom, performed by the "natural powers" used "freely and tranquilly" (*Ex.* 177), is merely one aspect of the election. In making the *Exercises*, we are led with Jesus in the ways of the Spirit. Then the election becomes the act through which a Christian who recognizes in himself the action of the Spirit incorporates in his own human life the act of Christ who, in little and great circumstances, accomplishes the will of the Father.

Two orders meet in an act performed in this way: that of human freedom and that of the action of the Holy Spirit. It is in the light of the latter that the act of freedom becomes an election: "The love that moves me and makes me choose a certain object should originate from above, from the love of God."

The election presupposes that our points of view are ordered in the light of, and through the motions of, the Holy Spirit. What I want is not primarily this particular object (whether marriage or priesthood), this particular mission, or this particular profession. I first of all want Jesus Christ, whom I recognize to have laid his hand upon me. The other things I want solely with that same will which first made me want Jesus Christ, and him alone. Moreover, in choosing this or that, I do not rely solely upon the work of my reason but also upon the action that the Spirit performs in me to make me feel his will, just as he did with Christ, who was "led by the Spirit".

What is the subject matter of the election?

According to some, it consists in deciding upon a state of life or a life's work, to the extent that these are recognized as implied in the Kingdom or the quest for the Kingdom. There is nothing like the *Exercises* for making this kind of choice and the commitment implied in it with full clarity, or better, for putting oneself in the attitude for such a choice whenever the day for it arrives.

For those who have no particular choice to make, the election consists in a more conscious and free adherence to the most essential thing in our life – a more personal appropriation of a vocation into which we can never enter fully enough.

At any rate, the important thing is the fundamental attitude requisite for the election. The *Exercises* lead us to rediscover this attitude, to guarantee that the choices made in our everyday life are made in harmony with God and with docility to the Holy Spirit.

In view of the practical affairs of daily life, this attitude is the entering into an ever-new order, that of the Spirit, about whom we know neither whence he comes nor where he goes but only that he is ceaselessly at work and that he is leading us. In order to let itself be led where it perhaps does not expect, our freedom makes itself receptive, as before a love that has been offered and recognized.

The election thus understood is very different from a resolution. Resolutions are practical decisions or applications that help us move in one direction or another. They belong to the moral order and help us persevere in an enterprise; but they are just as limited as that enterprise. We hardly need the entire spiritual preparation of the *Exercises* in order to make such resolutions. The advice of a few friends or a good self-examination are sufficient. Undoubtedly, these resolutions are not completely unrelated to the profound orientation of our life; they are a means of translating this orientation into everyday life. Yet they must not be confused with the election. Through the means it employs, the election guarantees the profound unity of the person that originates with the discovery of the action of the Holy Spirit.

Dispositions Requisite for the Election

Not everyone can make an election, just as not everyone can discern. A person's human qualities and his preparation are here more important than the decision he makes. It is the same in any human enterprise: the worth of the decision depends upon the man who makes it. And even when it is a question of constructing a spiritual edifice, no one can scrimp on this fundamental reality.

1. *Human Maturity*

There is a danger that some people will rely merely on their intellectual capacity. A person could discourse brilliantly about freedom and affective maturity – and still remain an adolescent. The first rule in this business is not to be overly impressed by anything – whether diplomas, reputation, jobs accomplished, or social prominence.

In order to make a real election, we must allow ourselves to recognize what we are. You want to decide, yet you cannot. You speak like books you have read or you repeat what you have heard from those around you. Dare, first of all, to create clarity within yourself. Without this, you will go round and round with all sorts of considerations, each of which has its value, but from which you will never escape, because they do not express what you are.

The retreat, to the extent that it calls the whole man into play, can open your eyes. Often, you will obtain the same result through a regular conversation with a counsellor about the experience you have had. The contact with daily reality, with an environment other than your own, or with different conditions of life are equally helpful for gaining some clarity about yourself – *if* you know what you expect from these contacts. For they constitute primarily an experiment for coming to know yourself and open yourself. In this search, it is helpful to benefit from the means that the sciences of psychology and sociology today put at your disposal.

It would be sheer foolishness to expect miracles or sudden changes from these means. Getting our lives in order demands time, even if we get a late start at it. How many people say: I am not comfortable in this profession, or, the decision was not ripe when I made it. Consequently, they decide to change their state. The important thing in a case like this is, first of all, to change myself, beginning with what I can see right now. I discover that I am an adolescent in the priesthood; well, marriage in itself is not going to make me more mature.

Is it possible to define the human maturity requisite for a true choice? Very empirically, let us say that a person can claim to have attained it if he has got a distance from his parents, his educators, those who influence him – not in rejection or pure criticism, but in the desire to take his own place among men. There is in true maturity a kind of modesty and an absence of sectarianism. In this connection, let us add the absence of panic in the face of one's own affective reactions: I neither deny them nor take them to be the last word. I accept them as a fact. This attitude differs from a pretentious self-control that is frequently accompanied by naïveté and contempt for others.

Without this natural development, there is the danger that a purported exercise of spiritual discernment might lead to chaos and illusion. No spiritual life can develop on the basis of an ignorance or rejection of nature.

2. *Correctness, or Purity, of Motivation*

In order to determine our choice, it is not enough that the proposed object be good. It is not enough even to recognize our capability to undertake it or the generous desires that it awakes in us. Not every good that presents itself is to be done. It is important that I discover the quality of the motives that are driving me. Sometimes we undertake a good action for wrong or mixed motives – secret fear, self-seeking. "If your eye is healthy, then your whole body is in the light; but if it is sick, then your body too is in the darkness" (Lk. 11:34). "In every good election," says St. Ignatius, "to the extent that it depends upon us, the eye of our intention ought to be simple" (*Ex.* 169).

As a catalyst for this necessary purification, St. Ignatius proposes a curious meditation, the one called "The Three Groups of Men, in order to embrace the best" (*Ex.* 150–7). It is not enough to possess a sum of money legitimately in order to have a peaceful soul; the young rich man is the perfect example of this. We must possess it "with correctness and purity, for the love of God". How many people deprive themselves of every comfort, busy themselves with the works of God, speak of justice and love for others – and yet are doing merely what they want. The proof of this is their difficulty when things do not turn out as they had planned. They never get to the bottom of things; or, if they try to, it is in order to twist the will of God to fit their own desires. The only people who really serve God with an upright heart are those who are not "even attached to keeping or not keeping the goods they have acquired". They want solely to keep it "in accordance with what God our Lord puts into their will and if it seems to them to be the best for the praise and service of his divine Majesty" (*Ex.* 155). What they are trying to reach in this act of choosing are the secret motives of their action.

Just to note it in passing, I feel that this kind of ideal can be proposed only to humanly balanced persons. What for them will be a source of freedom in action will be for others an occasion of incessant worries; for the latter will never consider themselves pure and ready enough. I should add that this disposition is not acquired overnight; it is the work of an entire lifetime. Father Lallemant, who made this the foundation of his "Spiritual Doctrine", proposed it to Jesuits at the end of their formation. The examination of conscience, as I have proposed it and as I will present it at the end of these ten days, is a means for maintaining this disposition day after day.

3. *Openness to Love*

This purification is not possible except as the consequence of the dynamism of love; it cannot be the result of a dry effort or of a rigorous examen. Thus, in order to permit these incessant "passings beyond" towards love, at the heart of the election just as at the heart of life, St. Ignatius presents, at the very moment of choice, another consideration, known by the name of the "three kinds of humility" (*Ex.* 164). They are, in reality, three stages along the road of love.

Beyond an interiorized fidelity (the first degree), beyond a purification that is applied to the roots of our desires in order to remain in a total transparency to the Spirit (the second degree), there is what St. Ignatius calls the third degree of humility. This is in fact the folly of a love that no longer has any rules. The love of the Father is manifested in the Son to the point of complete annihilation: Jesus made himself like the mankind he loved. This is the love of the servant, who did not seek to have the reputation of being just, but simply sought to be just. With Christ, who reveals and lives love, we no longer seek to attain a personal perfection, but rather to do everything "for the service and praise of the divine Majesty". The greatest glory of God, manifested in the face of Christ, becomes the sole concern of the "enamoured soul" (St. John of the Cross); and this marks the ultimate development of the Poor Man and of the Child described in the Beatitudes.

Through this triple disposition, a person lives with equilibrium under the impulse of the Spirit. It is an equilibrium constantly in motion. The equilibrium that establishes itself between two persons who love one another with genuine love can give us some idea of the love that is realized here: both have the same will, one and the same mind, the same way of feeling. It is a perfect resemblance. With this basis, almost without thinking about it, the best choices are made.

How to Make an Election

There is a danger that someone who just happens to open this book will immediately latch upon precisely this question. In fact, it is secondary when compared with the questions concerning preparations and dispositions. Even if an angel of God would come to assure you of God's will, in such a way that you could have no doubt about it, you should still be cautious. There is the inspiration, and there is the way of receiving it. The first does not depend upon you, but the second does. Therefore, never stop growing within yourself and purifying your heart in love.

It is over a period of time, says St. Ignatius, that "a healthy and good election" is made; that is, in a sequence of states, of desires, of thoughts. It is in progressing through this succession that we come to know the will of God.

There is the first type of election. It happens in the instant. God, "who enters, who leaves, who produces motions in the soul, who attracts it completely to the love of his divine Majesty" (*Ex.* 330), "moves and attracts the will" in such a way that it is impossible to doubt the origin of this movement (*Ex.* 175). The presence and action of God need no proof other than themselves. Why seek further? The absoluteness of God, who acts in the person "without intermediary" (*Ex.* 15), draws, "without doubt or the possibility of doubt", the person who has not stopped readying himself for this action. In this case, the only thing that is demanded of the person's fidelity is not to confuse this action of God with the application that the person unsuspectingly can make of it. Thus, we must simultaneously receive it with joy and remain vigilant.

In the second type, we are seized over the course of days and months by desires that pass, disappear, and come to life again, by attractions and repugnances – or, to use the language of the *Exercises*, "the experience of consolations and desolations". This is the most frequent case. Many people distrust this type, because it is dealing with feelings, "of good and bad angels". Even if this way of speaking surprises us and demands transposition into another language, there is still an undeniable reality here. St. Ignatius invites us to make a discernment about precisely this reality.

This discernment can take place only if we maintain the dispositions mentioned above – in short, only within the movement of the life of the Spirit. It consists in noting the effects of our feelings and desires as they progressively unfold in our experience. It is by examining the duration and quality of the desire that, one day, the evidence will be given to me. What comes from the demon remains hard, excites the imagination, demands hasty fulfilment; for the demon rejects time. This is the source of so many false vocations and false inspirations, even when they are directed towards good objects. The way of the Spirit, even if it shakes us, even if the object it presents to us produces repugnance or flight, is, in the last analysis, peace for the person, confidence in God, openness to others. You will recognize a good tree by its fruits (Mt. 7:15–19).

In order to exercise discernment, it is good to reinvigorate in our lives what we might call the "constants of God", those points or objects towards which the Spirit seems to lead us during the more calm periods of our existence. When the time for decision comes, we merely consent to that for which the past has been preparing us all along.

In the third type, there is nothing. There is no movement leading in one direction or the other. We nevertheless have to act. Thus, we can make an election through a discernment we might call moral or rational, by "using our natural powers with freedom and peace" (*Ex.* 177).

Even here where I have no light from above, I must make sure that I see things in harmony with God. Thus, in this decision which can remain open to criticism, the important thing is the way I make and live this decision: in relation to the absoluteness of God, which relativizes everything, and in the dispositions of peace and openness, which guarantee that I am on the path of God.

Naturally, I should carry on this work of reflection in a spirit of prayer, a type of prayer that situates me in one of those critical moments of life, where our vision is more lucid and impartial. St. Ignatius gives two examples of these limit-situations: how would I counsel a friend who found himself in a situation like mine? At the moment of death, what would I like to have done?

These three times are not opposed to one another. There can be a movement from one to another, in ascending or descending order. Often, in order to make a decision, we have no recourse but to the third: we are without light, and yet a decision must be made quickly. But the effort at impartiality and the atmosphere of prayer that surround this third time can bring about in us those "movements of spirits" or those "consolations" which confirm that God accepts the choice we make (*Ex.* 183). Inversely, the unexpected surge of light from God "without intermediary" (*Ex.* 15) and "without antecedent cause" (*Ex.* 330) does not dispense us from a recourse to discernment and to reflection, in order to guarantee that we have not been duped by our own interpretations and feelings.

We must make two remarks before examining a few applications:

Whatever the object of the election, it is important that, when the time comes to examine it, we persevere in an atmosphere of deep prayer. That is why I continue to contemplate, as I did earlier, the mysteries of the Gospel, those of the public life. In particular, I should often return to the great prayer of the Standards, the request to "be received with him".

Let us note also that, if a valid election is the kind that springs from the depths of freedom and takes shape in the secret of the heart, it should nevertheless be made before a witness, a spiritual counsellor. According to Ignatius, he "should not turn or lean towards one side or the other; rather, balancing himself like a scale between the two sides, he should let the Creator deal directly with his creature, and the creature with his Creator and Lord" (*Ex.* 15).

Many people would like to find a practical and definite way of resolving with certitude the various problems life brings their way. We have so much to do, they say, that we do not have time to reflect. You specialists should give us some simple means of seeing clearly. They forget that the search for the will of God can dispense no one from taking his time and putting his intelligence to work. Before making a discernment about anything at all, they ought to place themselves before the data of the problem and examine their various aspects. Besides, before any actual search, it is good to realize that, for persons who are still rather immature, a concern about accomplishing the will of God can become a source of agitation and kill their activity instead of helping it along. In these matters, nothing can dispense a person from the use of common sense and the suggestions of a few friends. In other words, before applying the rules for discernment, a person should ask himself if, in the matter facing him, it is really the place to make an election in the sense we have used the word and if he has the ability to make such an election.

1. *The Choice of a State of Life*

Without wanting to fix arbitrarily the moment when one should make such a choice, we could say that the time of a retreat – and especially this stage of the retreat – is the most favourable. When the time comes, and while taking into account the various suggestions given in these pages, it could be useful to answer – in writing, in order to fix one's ideas – the following questions:

1) Do I think I have sufficient maturity to decide freely? What indications make me doubt this maturity?

2) With which graces has God blessed me, beginning with my childhood? It is always good to trace the main lines of God's history in my life. The meditation of remembrance, indicated later, can help in this.

3) Concretely, what do I want right now? In the light of the retreat, how do I judge this desire? What effects are produced

in me by a rejection of it? By an acceptance of it?

4) What obstacles coming from myself, from others, from circumstances seem to block its realization?

Is there a consideration that seems to pull me more in one direction than in another? In my judgment, what value should be given to this consideration?

5) What is the reaction of those who know me to the desire I have?

Naturally, the answers to these questions should be formulated in tranquillity and especially in prayer. Without both of these conditions, it is impossible to preserve the correct vision and the unselfishness of the heart in the course of this search. If fatigue and turmoil should arise, it is better to stop the examination and to return to prayer.

2. Changing a State of Life

Here we are not speaking of those daily decisions which constitute the constant adaptation to a changing event. In order for the decision made then to continue to fit God's plan for our lives and for the world, the best means is the examination of conscience as I present it at the end of this book. Understood properly, it keeps alive, day after day, the necessary dispositions for a good election.

We shall not dwell too long on those decisions that we are led to make from time to time and which modify the course of our existence. An invitation that comes from outside, an unexpected event, a desire that has been working in us for a long time – these things push us towards new commitments. These cases should be treated like the preceding choice of a state of life. These choices are normal, concerning matters in which a previous election can always be changed. They belong to that ordinary fidelity which we try to maintain towards God's plan, whether in big or little matters.

The case is different (and it occurs often today) when we are dealing with a choice that of itself is definitive and yet concerning which the person who made it comes to conclude that he made a mistake. I was not mature enough to make that decision. I was under the influence of pressures and conditioning. It is a matter of authenticity, people think, to put everything into question. Moreover, add some people, it is questionable whether a lifelong commitment is really possible. Situations change, and so the choice should be reviewed.

Neither blind and voluntaristic fidelity on the one hand nor a hasty change on the other is the proper solution in such cases. Faced with the fact that I have lost the certitude that I am situated within the will of God, the question is: how can I rediscover his will in truth and in peace? Theoretical discussions, bitter brooding about the past, and the hope of sudden institutional changes are of no help here. Even if they seem to be right, these things mislead those who expect a solution from outside and not from an interior transformation of themselves, beginning with the concrete situation in which they live. I will make use of the situation in which I am involved in order to grow in a freedom which I consider to have remained immature. It is from a personal change – from the reform of my own life, as the *Exercises* would put it – that I must expect my primary light. It is a change that should occur simultaneously on two levels, the human and the spiritual, and which, on both of these levels, develops in the same direction: getting outside oneself in order to give oneself more entirely, "to leave one's self-love, one's own desires and interests" (*Ex.* 189). It is hard to imagine what good it would do a person to discourse about the universe and other people and yet not seek first of all to put his own life in order. He cannot help but remain unsatisfied, bitter, and disquieted. This shows that, in the actual living of his life, he is not in harmony with the plan of God.

In such a search, the help of a humane and impartial spiritual counsellor is more necessary than ever. The person who, under the pretext of autonomy, wants to solve his problems alone cannot help but merely become more engulfed in them. This fraternal assistance will help him withstand the shock of having his previous equilibrium collapse. Thrown into question, but standing alone, a person runs the risk of destroying himself even more. If, on the other hand, he accepts the necessity of this long and painful journey, which he at times regrets not having made earlier, he discovers that there is no other way for him to find God in peace.

Thus, *either* this long effort (about which the person making it sometimes wonders *how* or even *if* it will end) becomes the occasion for experiencing, more and more frequently and deeply, moments of a real, hitherto unknown freedom. This is the sure sign that soon he will set out again unhesitatingly along the road that he had chosen earlier, but now for "pure, untarnished, and unmixed" motives (*Ex.* 172). *Or else* this effort, performed with uprightness of heart, succeeds only in making him more rigid and troubled. This is the sign that, despite his good will, the road he has been travelling is not for him and that he can leave it without fear. This, too, is a real choice. Even if he abandons a path that others or he himself at one time thought to be better, there is no infidelity involved. The peace that accompanies the decision is the proof.

In any case, when someone tells me, "I have lost my vocation", I first of all want to ask him, "Have you done all in your power to maintain the quality of life that would allow this vocation, if it is real, to develop?" A vocation is never finished once and for all. It is either disintegrating or growing. Inertia makes it disappear. Thus, if you experience repugnance for what you loved in the beginning, follow the counsel of St. Ignatius: beg the Lord to choose you for the object of your repugnance, "provided it be for the service and praise of his divine Goodness" (*Ex.* 157). The persistence of the repugnance in the face of the struggle against it is a clear indication that God's will does not lie here. If, however, through and beyond this repugnance you discover peace and thus see the repugnance disappear, this is a sign that God will help you live out your vocation, even if you experience emotional resistance to it.

3. *Decisions in a Community*

The question of decisions made not by an individual but by a community seems new today. Actually, it goes back to the Acts of the Apostles, when the apostles met to decide on the choice of Matthias and on the mission of Paul and Barnabas. It occurs in the history of the Church each time that men ripe with the Spirit gather to work together. One example is the deliberation of the first companions of St. Ignatius about whether they should make permanent the union that existed among them.

For a community to be able to move together towards a decision, it seems that a certain number of conditions should be met, as in the case of an individual's election. First of all, on the human level. Such decisions cannot be made by people who do not know one another or by people among whom there remain latent conflicts. Here as elsewhere, personal relations are necessary. Then, on the spiritual level. This community in search of God's will should be united in the same spiritual and apostolic purpose. One and the same faith in Jesus and a community of vocation should constitute the essential relationship of its members.

In particular, this community should have the experience of common prayer. This is what disposes their hearts to be open to the Spirit and to others; and it guarantees for each person in the group the independence necessary for saying freely what seems right to him and for guarding himself against the unconscious pressures that can be at work. A retreat made together is one of the best ways of putting this common prayer into practice.

In the search for a decision, there will occur something like the three times we have already mentioned. Sometimes it is the inspiration that no one doubts: "Set Barnabas and Saul apart for me" (Acts 13:2). Sometimes it is a long discernment of desires and attractions experienced over a long period of time within the group, up to the day when the decision thrusts itself upon them. Finally, it is sometimes a fraternal discussion in which each person strives to offer a heart that is open and impartial to the different opinions as though to new calls, in order to arrive at the light. This discussion leads to a spiritual discernment only if it is not merely a free exchange of points of view but also a submission to the path taken by the Spirit in the hearts of all the members.

This prayer, as it becomes deeper, helps them go beyond the sometimes opposing expressions that the individuals give to the light received. The Spirit, as at Pentecost, permits them to discover, beyond the language differences, the reality lived by them collectively and as individuals.

As in the case of an individual's decisions, there can be no ready-made method. Here as elsewhere, there is the danger of wanting to go too fast, of forcing others to come around to our own way of thinking – fundamentally, of not renouncing ourselves enough to let God and other people exist.

In all the cases considered above, there comes a time to conclude the matter. It is not difficult if I have arrived at a clear choice – the discovery of a road to travel or the confirmation of a road already followed. What does it mean, however, if I discover that there is no clarity? Should I conclude that it was a failure? I will not be able to come to this conclusion if, checking the road travelled over these days, I carefully determine why I am no longer advancing. It is a real choice if I humbly recognize the real state of affairs, even if I must admit that, for the moment, I cannot choose in a clear and firm manner. The difficulties are not eliminated, but I see better how to bear them and how to proceed.

Should we write? A real election is an act that calls for writing only to the extent that it is a commitment, like the signature at the bottom of a contract. Writing also helps us make the object of choice more precise and helps us remember it. In this case, let us write without attaching undue importance to these lines. Otherwise, we would be undertaking literature; and then the words would grow old.

In conclusion, the important thing in all our human behaviour and in our various decisions is the direction of our intention: "In every good election, to the extent that it depends upon us, the eye of our intention should be clear" (*Ex.* 169). Concerning one and the same object, the choices will vary with the individuals. And for the same person, the choices will vary with the passage of life. The habit of discernment permits us, in all these different situations, to discover the signs of God, that is, how God accomplishes his Reign in everything and turns everything into good for those who love him. In all things, even when we are deprived of all certitude, this habit makes us return to the source.

1. *The Young Rich Man and Peter (Lk. 18:18–30)*

This episode confronts us with the fundamental dispositions for making a good election. It is no longer a question here of avoiding evil or of observing the commandments: I have kept them since my youth, says the young man. He possesses his riches legitimately: he has never stolen. But they are for him a cause of sadness: he is possessed by them instead of his possessing them. He is not free to love.

We are, with the invitation of Jesus, on the level of the most perfect, that is, on the level of love. These riches that bind you are merely means, and yet you have made them into an absolute. Abraham, the father of believers, did not do that: he did not refuse God his "sole" and legitimate son – not out of fear, not out of calculation, but with the certitude that the God who demanded this of him and who is faithful in his promises was "capable of resurrecting the dead" (Genesis 22:1–19 and Heb. 11:17–19). We stand before the absolute of a love that reconciles contraries. For him who believes, nothing is impossible for God.

The reaction of Peter confirms this. We have left everything, he says. We are tempted to say to him, "What have you left, Peter? A small house, a boat, fishing nets. . . ." What is that in comparison with the riches of the young man? For Jesus, the important thing is not the quantity but the quality of the gift, beginning with what we are and have. Why imagine some extraordinary situation?

The Lord who was saddened to see the young man depart was happy at the reaction of Peter. In truth, all those who do the same "receive much more in this age and eternal life in the age to come". Like Abraham, they recover on a new level, that of freedom and grace, what they consented to lose on the level of nature. Everything – even their dearest son – becomes for them a gift of God. It is through a commitment to "whoever loses gains" that they discover life and peace (Jn. 12:23–6).

Anyone who wants to attain these summits of love must struggle with God in prayer, as Jacob did at the ford of Jabbok (Gen. 32:23–33). "I will not leave you until you bless me." Man leaves this struggle lame, but free for life.

2. *The Grace of Discernment (St. John and St. Paul)*

Two images help us penetrate its nature: unction (1 Jn. 2:26–7) and touch (Phil. 1:2–11). An unction, like oil that a piece of clothing soaks up, fastens on to the core of a person with the truths already received (Jn. 14:26), in such a way that there is no more need to teach him about them. This knowledge, which is exercised with the spontaneity of an instinct, is given to the person who finds pleasure and sweetness in the law of God (Ps. 119[118]).

This discernment is part of the work accomplished by him who began it in us, looking forward to the coming of the Day of Christ. It cannot be isolated from that growth in charity which, for the Christian, is the source of true knowledge. This is the love that communicates the "refined touch that helps us discern the better". It makes us see what the closed heart does not see. Happy are the pure hearts; they see God (Mt. 5:8). A hardened heart blinds the eyes (Jn. 12:37–41). This discernment is the sign of the ripeness of the fruit we bear in Christ (Jn. 15:1–10).

It is not given to beginners, those who are still at the level of the "first rudiments of the oracles of God". It develops in those who advance to "the perfect instruction" and maintain themselves through the exercise of this sense in the "taste" of the heavenly gift and in the "sweetness" of the beautiful word of God (Heb. 5:11–6:8). It leads "towards true knowledge" the person who, having put on the new man, renews himself in the image of his Creator (Col. 3:10). Here the "judgment" repeats itself and permits the person to "discern" what is God's will, what is good, what pleases God, what is perfect" (Rm. 12:2).

It is through his fruits that the believer recognizes in himself the presence and action of the Spirit (Gal. 5:16–26): charity, joy, peace, . . . Not by the charitable work taken alone: the Pharisees and the pagans can do as much (Mt. 6:1–18); they have received their reward. The important thing is the way in which this work is accomplished; this makes it clear, in us as in Jesus, that the work comes from God (1 Cor. 13:1–7). Everything in the life of a Christian forms a whole; we cannot isolate this concern about discernment from the other instances of the Spirit's activity in our lives.

3. *Meditation on Memories*

The believer, as he goes through life, develops a memory for the marvels that God has accomplished in him, for his people, and in mankind. We could never list all the psalms of remembrance – cf. Pss. 105(104) and 106(105). In re-reading them, a person learns to recognize the ways of God.

Thus, each of us, in recalling the great moments of his life, discovers there are some constants. A thread ties them together, and the direction of this thread helps him discover the goal towards which God is leading him.

Such a meditation anticipates the "contemplation to obtain the love of God", which "recalls all the good things I have received". Through this grateful recognition, it leads us "to love and serve God in all things" (Exercises 230–7).

4. *The Spiritual Development of Peter*

There is a danger of making the election, like the retreat, into a rational undertaking. There we seek to regulate our problems simply through the computation of human motives. That is why it is good at this time to

plunge oneself into prayer. The great means for this prayer is the contem-
plation of the mysteries of the Lord's life, in particular of his apostolic
life. In keeping with the exercise of discernment, let us present some
scenes typical of the way in which Jesus called and led his apostles, in
particular Peter.

We could first of all note in a global way, following St. Ignatius's analysis (*Ex.* 275), some of the characteristics of the divine
vocation. The call makes itself heard progressively and with
extreme gentleness. It pays no attention to a man's worth or
merit; the "apostles were uneducated and lowly". Without
distinction, he addresses Philip, a simple man, Matthew, a
sinner and publican, just as he does the other apostles. All of
them are invited to receive gifts that elevate them beyond what
man can imagine; they are chosen to "be his companions" and,
hence, preachers and exorcists of demons (Mk. 3:13–19). Each
vocation binds together the littleness of man and the grandeur
of God in the gratuity of love.

Within the group of the apostles, Peter seems to be the object
of a particular formation. Look at the scenes that are connected
with him specifically. Thanks to them, we can follow his development:

Jn. 1:40	Jesus gazes at Peter.
Lk. 5:1–11	The "bewilderment" of Peter.
Jn. 6:67–71	To whom shall we go, Lord?
Mt. 14 to 17	The walking on water. The confession of Caesarea Philippi. The reprimand of Peter. The Transfiguration.
Mt. 17:24–7	Who pays the tax? The children or the strangers? The freedom of the sons.
Mt. 18:21–2	Universal pardon. How many times should we pardon?
Mt. 19:27–9	We have left everything for you. What will come of it? All of this before "being sifted" (Lk. 22:31–4).

Let us take our time on some of the more significant scenes of
Mt. 14 to 17. They describe Jesus's way of forming the apostle.

First of all, the test of faith: walking on water (Mt. 14:22–33).

Jesus goes off to pray alone while the storm is beginning to rage. The Lord leaves man to himself, to make him grow in faith. I made you walk in the desert . . . in order to test you . . . as a father corrects his child (Dt. 8:1–6). Man, left to himself and seized by fear, does not recognize God any longer; the disciples think they are seeing a ghost. The Lord's return teaches man "the understanding of hope in God" (St. Francis Xavier) and teaches him not to rely on himself. But the Lord purifies the faith of Peter even more. Spontaneously Peter requests: "If it is you, tell me to come to you." He sets out. Some impure elements again mix themselves into his confidence. He starts to rely upon himself and looks at his feet. He sinks. The Lord's reproach, effective like every word of God, produces a new faith in Peter's heart.

Especially the trilogy: confession, reprimand, transfiguration.

Peter receives the revelation of the Father. "This revelation comes to you from the Father," Jesus tells him. "No one comes to me unless the Father draws him" (Jn. 6:44–6). Peter is one of those little ones to whom the mysteries of God are revealed. Now he can become the witness of the faith, the rock upon which the believing Church will be built. Nothing can prevail against it.

But, as often happens with us, Peter believes rashly in what has happened. He speaks under the inspiration of the Spirit, but he does not yet realize the import of what he says. Thus, he is overcome by the first difficulty: that cannot happen to you, he tells Jesus after the prediction of his Passion. "Get behind me; you are a Satan for me. You do not have the thoughts of God, but of men." Brought back to his senses, Peter, to his great displeasure, must hear, along with the others: "If anyone wants to follow me, let him deny himself and take up his cross." We must always return to that point; a person recognizes Jesus as the Son of God only in the manifestation of his love, the cross. Peter still has a long way to go before he understands that.

Still, "six days later", Jesus manifests himself to Peter in the glory of the Father. At the time, Peter, reeling and not knowing what he is saying, experiences things that exceed his grasp. Everything is there all at once: the Exodus to be accomplished in Jerusalem (Lk. 9:31), the great witnesses, Moses and Eliah, the cloud, sign of God's presence. How does all this fit together? He will not understand it until later (Jn. 13:7). For the time being, looking up again, the only thing he sees is Jesus. He must go down the mountain, to set out for Jerusalem – again, without revealing anything about what has just happened.

Thus, in our own lives, we cannot understand right away what is happening to us. Reality is already there as a whole, but it remains confused. In order for the road to become clear, we must go through nights, perhaps even betrayals. But it is still the Lord who is leading us. Later we shall recall having heard then, as Peter did, the prophetic word; and we shall come to see it "as a lamp that shines in a darkened place, until day dawns" (1 Peter 1:12–21).

We can conclude the entire matter of the election with the following remark. Peter wants an immediate solution for the problems he encounters. At the level he remains, he cannot find absolute certitude. He must join Christ, "setting out resolutely for Jerusalem" (Lk. 9:51). Even after a decision made in this spirit, there can be at least apparent failure. But the important thing is to be sure, like Christ on his way to Jerusalem, that God wants it like this. What happens then does not concern me.

AT THE END OF THESE FOUR DAYS

The *Exercises*, especially those of the second stage, call into play the creative energies of a person, those which constitute his human personality, in order to submit them freely to the superior dynamism of the Spirit. There is a danger that certain people will be disturbed by this process. They are not in the habit of regulating their problems in life at this degree of depth.

They habitually stay at the level of reason and of human prudence.

The experience of the *Exercises* resembles, to a certain extent, what happens in an artist, a man of action, or a person in love. An activity takes place within him that does not depend upon him. If he wants to master it, he kills it, thereby killing the better part of himself. He must co-operate with this force that comes from elsewhere. In this work, reason has its place, but not its usual place. It gathers data, notes the results, compares them among themselves; but it is incapable of foreseeing what the person will be asked to live out. It prepares the way for the decision but falls short of the decision. It is at the service of something that exceeds it. At times transported outside himself, at times totally bewildered, the person who is the centre of all this interior labour clears himself a path towards the unknown, until the day the evidence is there. Once again, he cannot clutch the evidence as his possession, under pain of drying up the sources of the inspiration. A new and incessant fidelity is demanded of him. This fidelity, once accepted, leads him to new adventures, new creations. This is how it is with a person grasped by the Holy Spirit: "What sort of life have I got myself into?" he asks himself, along with St. Ignatius. The vocation that keeps moving him forward is not like a programme to be accomplished but rather like a continual invitation to fidelity.

Is everyone capable of undertaking such an adventure? It seems that St. Igantius thought not. With certain persons, he says, "one should not involve them in the question of the election" (*Ex.* 18). To the extent that those who show a great natural capacity and great spiritual desire will find in this method a liberation that will help them live and act, to that same extent others with less capacity risk finding there nothing but complications and disturbances.

The peace involved in self-acceptance seems to be the supreme norm here. The *Exercises*' method for making an election is merely a means. Like counsels lavished upon someone who wants to be creative or to love, this method can help only that person who is capable of submitting himself to it. What is helpful for one person can be harmful, or at least incomprehensible, to another. "Each person receives from God his particular gift – one person receives from God this gift, another that gift" (1 Cor. 7:7). What permits all of them to discover their unanimity is not an identity of paths followed but their mutual respect in the incomparable love of Christ. The path that fits the individual is that which allows him to acquire the freedom to love genuinely and to recognize in himself and in others the universal grace of God.

The important thing for each person, in the discovery of his own path, is that he does not remain torn in different directions, in uncertainty and discontentment, but that he leave satisfied, having found "what can help and be of more profit" (*Ex.* 18). Efficacy, humility, and peace are bound together. Consequently, the only similarity shared by all these people, in the midst of their diversity, is that they are all disciples of Jesus.

Whatever conclusion we reach at the end of this second stage, the goal has been reached if each person has worked through the bitterness of finding himself other than his dream-self or, on the contrary, has worked through his complacency with what he has already accomplished. In these conflicting situations, we come to realize that we cannot accomplish the will of God unless we go beyond what we are and the way we live at the present time. We rediscover, though at a greater depth, the dilemma we were caught in at the end of the first stage (pp. 76–8). Either you are in peace; then remain vigilant. Or you are not; then work to rediscover it. You will not advance unless you agree not to stop and focus upon yourself. St. John would say: either your heart condemns you; then recall that "God is greater than your heart and knows all things". Or it does not condemn you; then turn yourself even more completely towards God, to whom you have free access (1 Jn. 3:20–1). Through Christ, enter into the paschal mystery, the mystery of the passage.

THIRD STAGE:
Christ Living in the Church

Having glimpsed the attitude that permits the election, can we stop here? The experience of the life of the Spirit cannot limit itself to the discovery of an interior equilibrium, even if it were the most dynamic in the world. Man makes himself into something only that he might give himself. The person who lives in the Spirit, like him who is seized by the inspiration of genius or by love, cannot shut himself up within himself. Whoever wants to save his life must lose it (Mt. 16:25).

The more the spiritual life deepens, the more it calls man beyond himself, to help him attain the dimensions of the universal Christ. Beginning with the election, the goal of this last stage is to make us live the "expansion of heart" of a man who has let himself be grasped by the mystery of Christ. Like every other form of life, the spiritual life develops in the tension of two opposing movements, centripetal and centrifugal. Summoning man into his most intimate depths, the spiritual life is, however, never a solitary adventure.

In practice, man experiences this law of life as a wrenching of his being. On the one hand, his concern for a personal life closes him upon himself and alienates him from the masses; on the other hand, the desire to give himself to all men soon leads him to serve merely an abstract humanity. How can he be simultaneously personal and universal? Theoretically, this is possible to resolve. In practice, in both cases, man runs up against his limit – let's call it his sin. Christ alone removes the limit and lives the reconciliation in him. The meditation of these three days confronts me with this reconciliation. Christ is simultaneously the one who knows me in my most intimate being and the one in whom I rediscover all men. This is the mystery of his body. Identically, it is the mystery of the Church.

In this mystery, I am simultaneously at the goal and at the

source of every spiritual life. At the goal, because all my efforts aim at confronting me with the choice of Christ on the way to his Passion, that of living the love of the Father to the very end. At the source, because I cannot be faithful to any choice at all nor grow in it unless I am already drinking from the living springs of the Body and Blood of Christ.

At this stage, I also grasp the double character of every spiritual life in Christ – spiral and sacramental. At each stage, it is always a question of the same elements, but each time at a more profound degree of unity. This unity I attain in the Body of Christ, where the earthly reality becomes the sign of another, invisible reality, in whom all things hold together.

The coming days, by introducing me into these mysteries, make me enter a new stage of prayer: a prayer more simple, more unified, more contemplative, more unselfish, and yet paradoxically closer to action and everyday life.

This, as a matter of fact, makes prayer more disconcerting and sometimes more difficult. This prayer demands a more total loss of self, a more profound and peaceful concentration on the mystery of the other. A person who is agitated, distracted, or tense lets the grace slip away. We are asked to try our hand at it, so that we might glimpse the marvels we are called to live and which, in the words of the final contemplation of the *Exercises*, will help us find God in all things.

VIII.   The Gift of His Body:
The Eucharist

Everything I experience in my life passes into Christ. This
passage occurs every day in the Eucharist. The Spirit who sanc-
tified the body of Christ and glorified it through the resurrection now transforms my members, my body, my action and
gives them eternal life through the Lord's gift of his body to me.
In the Eucharist, I discover the dimensions of all human existence, of mine and of all other men's. It is no longer I who live.
. . . Your bodies are the members of Christ. The Church is
built up through the Eucharist.

Today's prayer invites me to establish the place of the sacrament in my spiritual life. Through this sacrament, everything I
do becomes the occasion for a continual exchange of love. I give
him what I am; he gives me what he is. This exchange already
took place in the sacrament of penance. Yet it is not only evil
that Christ takes up to change into good; it is also the strengths
of our life, in order to bring them, in him, to their fulfilment;
and it is also all those diverse charismata that the Spirit distri-
butes in order to build up the Church.

How did it ever happen that, for so many years of Christian
life, we saw the Eucharist merely as one practice or devotion
among others? It is the centre of all. It is the Eucharist that
makes the Christian a martyr; that is, a man who bears witness,
at the heart of the mortal life that is his, to the eternal life he
receives in Christ.

How should we pray when confronted with this mystery?

In the peacefulness of our affectivity and our mind, in which
the preceding days have established us, we now should simply
taste the love of the Lord. We arrive, as the various authors tell
us, at the third stage of the spiritual life: how it is merely a
question of union. See and taste.

As we soon discover, prayer changes. It is no longer so much a contemplation in order to gather lessons from Our Lord, but rather contemplation in order to adore, ask, tell of our love, thank, or say nothing. This prayer has no other usefulness than to make us exist in him and with him – better, to gladden us with what he is and what he is doing. The Lord exists for me, for all men; and that is enough for me.

Faced with prayer of this kind, which we sometimes feel to be too elevated and almost suffocating, we can merely become like the "little poor boy" Ignatius mentions in the contemplation of the Nativity: he is allowed into a brilliant feast without any idea of how he should behave. We can only offer our helplessness, our services, and our desires.

The result of the election, we said, was an abandonment of self and an acceptance of the other. It is not necessary to wait long in order to live this out. This prayer before the Eucharist is the right occasion for it.

Naturally, the suggestions for prayer and the directions become simpler; they are now merely a commentary on the mystery or on the text. The individual, having read them, should feel free to follow the movement of the Spirit in his prayer.

Helps for Today's Prayer

More than ever before, we should use a text only to the extent that it maintains our attention in prayer. What we want is to be able to taste the Reality beneath the sign. The texts concerning the Eucharist help us to discover this Reality.

1. *The "Grand Entrance": The Washing of the Feet (Jn. 13)*

The solemnity of tone introduces the simplest of gestures: on the one hand, the announcement of the great passage and of the consummation of love; on the other, the washing of feet. Within the perspectives of the work that Jesus is accomplishing, the least gesture takes on an immense significance. "Do you understand what I have done for you?" That is how it is with the least expression of tenderness in our human relationships.

The Creator puts himself at the feet of his creature, to teach him simultaneously how he is loved and how he ought to love. Jesus puts himself at the feet of each of us. Peter cannot stand this. Nevertheless, Jesus must leave us alone, so that we might "understand later". From now on, man can no longer despise himself or his brother. Whatever you do to the least of these little ones, you have done to me. Each man becomes Jesus for me.

In order to rediscover him, when he goes away without my being able to follow him immediately, I am given the commandment of fraternal love. This is the sign that I belong to him and that he is with us (vv. 33–5). The epistle of John develops this presence of God in the love we have for one another (1 Jn. 4:12).

Peter, impatient as usual, remains at the door of this mystery. He defends himself as unworthy. "Allow yourself to do it", or rather, "Allow me to do it", Jesus tells him. "You will understand only later." Still this "later", which echoes the "behind me". Peter would like to march at the very front. He will have so much difficulty in admitting soon that "You will follow me later" (v. 36). The education of Peter continues; he must allow his master to be the first traveller on the path of love. It is not we who made him, but he who made us. He loved us first.

These gestures and words of love take place and are heard in an atmosphere of final judgment: Satan has already entered into the heart of Judas. He leaves and it is night. Nevertheless Jesus exults: the Son of Man has been glorified. It is the moment of the great betrayal and of the definitive act of sharing. Jesus, by plunging into evil, has emptied it of its power.

All of these actions and feelings, which make me penetrate to the heart of the mystery, show me the context in which I should offer the Eucharist.

2. *The Gift of His Body (Lk. 22:1–20)*

St. Luke, in recounting the preparations for the paschal meal, gives me the dimensions of the Last Supper. The real drama takes place in the heart and in the realm of the invisible. Satan is the protagonist, the Prince of this world, whom the Word-made-flesh has come to cast out of the heart of his creature. Especially, it is the work of freedom. Jesus sets a scene that shows he is not taken by surprise by the events: "Go into the city," he tells Peter and John, "and you will find . . ." He knows what he is going to do and what is going to happen to him (Jn. 18:4). I give my life when I want to; I will take it up again when I want to. This is the life which he receives from the Father and which he returns to him, when the hour has come.

Moreover, Jesus freely inserts himself within the context of human history. He performs the Last Supper on the anniversary of the Passover and the Exodus. This insertion gives meaning to his gesture: the Eucharist is a Passover, a passage, and a meal for travellers. In the age we live in, the body of Christ is the viaticum of eternal life. He comes down into time in order to lead us with him until the end of time.

Jesus freely shows his love by the gift of his body. I have desired with a great desire to eat this Passover. This is my body, given up for you. For a man, the body is his means of expressing himself; it is that which sets him off from the rest of the universe, as well as that through which he immerses himself in the universe. It is, above all, the means for translating the love he bears in his heart: he speaks himself through gestures, he gives himself in union and in death. Jesus gives his body to signify the exchange of love that occurs between him and us. The body of Jesus belongs no longer to himself but to me; my body belongs no longer to myself but to him. The mutual gift that a man and wife make of their bodies to signify the love within them is the image of the mutual gift that Christ and we make of our bodies. "Offer your persons as living victims, holy and agreeable to God; that is spiritual worship" (Rm. 12:1). "Your body is a temple of the Holy Spirit . . .; you do not belong to yourself. Glorify God in your body" (1 Cor. 6:19–20). And in this exchange of love, he communicates to our mortal bodies the immortality of his body. "He was not abandoned to the underworld, nor did his body see corruption" (Acts 2:31). He gives his body so that we might have the life that is in him, that of the Father and of the Spirit.

This gift is the new covenant, the definitive covenant. His sacrifice makes all others useless – those of the pagans, those of the Old Testament, and all those which men make to save mankind. Those sacrifices are in vain, for they are incapable of delivering from death. He, offered up in love and raised by the Spirit, enters by his blood "into heaven, before the face of God" (Heb. 8 and 9). His sacrifice is the sole sacrifice, because it is a victory sacrifice. If we, along with him, freely offer our mortal bodies in love, it is so that, through him, we may be clothed in immortality. Through the victorious cross, a new meaning is given to the sacrifices performed by men. Consecrating the body of Christ and proclaiming his death, we enter into his victory.

3. *The Memorial: The Breaking of the Bread (Acts 2:42) and the Lord's Supper (1 Cor. 11:17-34)*

This gift is given to us in the humblest Eucharist gathering, wherever some disciples of Jesus gather together for the breaking of the bread. What have we made out of the Lord's Last Supper? A practice, an official rite, an ordinary meal, the occasion of arguments, . . .? To do so is to despise the Church of God, says Paul. You have made it the showplace for your divisions and inequalities. Don't you have your houses for eating and drinking?

Our common meal is the Lord's Supper. Each time we take part in it, we announce his death, until he comes. Our gathering today refers itself to that day on which the Lord gave his body and blood, while at the same time it announces the day when his entire body will be reunited in him. The triple dimension of the Eucharist: today, the death of Jesus, the day of his coming. The Lord is in the midst of his disciples gathered together. No doubt it is inevitable that schisms break out among them. Nevertheless, what a scandal it is that the Lord's gift be disgraced among us!

The Lord's Last Supper, like his death, constitutes a real judgment. There each person shows from which spirit he comes. He eats and drinks to his own condemnation if he fails to discern there the body. To discern the body means to recognize simultaneously the Head and the members, he who unites and we who are united. Whoever fails to recognize both in the breaking of the bread will answer for the body and the blood of the Lord. If, when you come to the altar, you remember that your brother has something against you, go first to reconcile yourself with him (Mt. 5:23-4). In a Christian gathering, the teaching of the apostles, the fraternal sharing, the breaking of the bread and the prayer all go hand in hand (Acts 2:42).

Thus the Church is formed through the Eucharist. The entire context of the Epistle to the Corinthians, where Paul speaks of the Lord's Supper, is an ecclesiastical context. The foundation of the Church is the faith in the one Lord, not an attachment to Paul, Cephas, or Apollo. And that which manifests the Church is the life of the Spirit in the variety of charismata and the unity of charity. It is from this starting point that each individual resolves the questions that arise during the course of the community's existence: the scandal of incest, recourse to pagan courts, the life-style within marriage, virginity, social conditions, meat offered to idols, the order within assemblies, etc.

What we are looking for each time we come together is to grow in the life of the Spirit, whose dimensions are shown to us during the Lord's Supper. Again, it is the body of the Lord that grounds our faith in the universal resurrection (1 Cor. 15).

The meaning of the eucharistic gathering, such as Paul presents it in the First Letter to the Corinthians, corrects the various abuses that threaten Christian worship. This worship can be nothing other than that spiritual worship, described by Chapter 12 of the Epistle to the Romans, which gathers up all existence and blossoms into universal love. Through the body of Christ has come the hour when "the true worshippers worship the Father in spirit and truth" (Jn. 4:23).

4. *Flesh and Spirit (John 6)*

Meditation on Chapter 6 of the Gospel of St. John is another way to penetrate the richness of the body and blood of Christ. In this connection, it is good to recall the counsel: we should not look for the logical sequence of these thoughts; rather, we should let ourselves be penetrated by them so that their unity appears to us, a unity that is spiritual.

This body that he gives, and which the Jews think was born of Joseph, is the work of the Spirit. That is why it gives life to the world. It has a certain power because of the mystery of his birth: born of the Virgin through the operation of the Spirit. Every man who is born comes into the world through human generation. Mortal man can communicate only what he has, a life marked by death. In the midst of this cycle of mortal generations, there appears this flesh that the Word assumed in the freedom of love. Moreover, this flesh, which makes him like us, brings to our flesh life and immortality. Whoever eats my flesh will live for ever. The Spirit is in my flesh.

The Lord himself is Spirit (2 Cor. 3:17).

This life is received in faith. Just as the flesh that gives this life was conceived in the faith of Mary, so also it produces its effect in us through faith. The work of God is that you believe in him whom God sent. "No one comes to me unless the Father draws him." Man does not reach God except in the flesh of his Son. Yet this flesh communicates to us the life of the Father only if it is recognized in the Spirit. The flesh is of no use; it is the Spirit that gives life. The Jews recognized only the flesh of the son of Joseph, and the Lord's manner of speaking scandalizes them. Only those who hear the Father's teaching recognize simultaneously the flesh and the Spirit.

153

This flesh produces its grace in them; it is a sign of union with the Spirit. The life of the Father is communicated to them. Just as I am living through the Father, so the person who receives my flesh lives through me. There takes place in him a divine assimilation, a transfiguration of his mortal self into Christ. The life of the Father is given to him, communicated by the Son and lived in the Spirit. This life is the life of the world. Through his flesh that has been glorified and given to us, Christ draws the universe along with him. What will you say when you see the Son of Man ascending to where he was before?

Who can stand such claims? This language is too strong. The exchange that takes place in the flesh of the Word incarnate is a scandal for the mind: God in the flesh, abiding among us. It is the scandal of the continuation of the Word incarnate; "We will hear you some other time on this matter," the Athenians say, after hearing about the resurrection of the dead (Acts 17:32). It is only the faith of the little ones, to whom the Father delights in revealing himself (Lk. 10:21), that surpasses every limit and accepts, along with Peter, the gift of God: "To whom shall we go? You have the words of eternal life."

5. *The Discourse After the Last Supper (Jn. 14 to 17)*

It is in the light of the body of Christ that we should read "all the words of love there are in Scripture" (Bossuet). The most burning words are those reported by John after the institution of the Eucharist. They can serve as an accompaniment or as a thanksgiving for the prayer of this day.

We could let these mysterious words of the Lord drop one by one into our heart, following the suggestions given earlier on the method of prayer: with an attentive and peaceful heart, with the body drawn into a unity, and to the rhythm of our breathing. The word of the Lord, read in faith, unites us with him.

In the same way, we can take up the prayer of the Psalms and sing them in the context of the Eucharist: the Psalms of the history of Israel, or of the desire for God, or of the creation. The liturgy continually invites us to do this.

This way of praying teaches us about gratuity in prayer. The person anxious about deriving profit from everything ends up getting nothing, unless he consents simply to exist in the presence of God and receive his mystery, according to the measure of grace that is given him at the present time.

IX. At the Sources of Being and Life: The Passion

In the contemplation on the Passion, we reach the goal of all spiritual effort: joining Jesus in the act of freedom through which he offers up his life and his death in order to accomplish the will of the Father, the glorification of all mankind in his body. Baptism commits us to this effort, but it is not yet accomplished.

In him, our daily death finds its meaning. It too becomes, in turn, an act of freedom: I give my life when I want to; I take it up when I want to. Because he lived it freely in love, without returning hatred to those who killed him, he has, through his death, brought victory over the world and sin. The real victory consists in undergoing death in freedom and love: "dying for the unjust" (Rom. 5). But who can do this? (Rom. 5). Only one, he who died for us when we were completely without righteousness. Through his death, our liberation begins: "Having become one identical being with him through a death like his", "we are already living a new life" (Rom. 6).

The meditation on the Passion enlightens not only life and death but all our preoccupations. We can accept all of them, especially those concerning our faith, in the light of the Passion. The Passion makes us accept suffering not only for the Church but also because of the Church. It gets down to the roots of our temptations to triumphalism and discouragement. It makes us go beyond the narrow love that we can have for even the holiest things – our apostolic works, our communities, the Church. Before the Passion, my pride in self crumbles; and nothing is left but the love of the suffering Just Person who gives himself completely.

Many questions about the world and the Church simply disappear in the light that streams from the cross. No part of human suffering is denied; yet everything is drawn beyond that. Thus, although we find ourselves beyond our strength, the Passion remains a school of life.

Fundamentally, we are trying to rediscover in prayer what the first Christians discovered there; for their faith helped them discover the glorious cross. From the cross, the disciple of Jesus draws the strength and the joy requisite for witnessing. It is not that he claims to be doing something for Christ; rather, he knows himself to have been chosen by his master to manifest in his mortal flesh the power of the Spirit, which first erupted in the flesh of the Lord, put to death by men and glorified by the Spirit.

The Prayer Before the Passion

This prayer, like that of the sinner, can be made only in the depths. Otherwise, just as the prayer of the sinner risked staying at the level of the law and of moral fault, so this prayer risks being a mere sentimental pitying, a search for rational explanations, a concern to imitate. Like the meditation on sin, this meditation is fruitful only if it makes us meet Jesus Christ in order to place ourselves alongside him at the roots of being and love.

In order to reach us in these depths, this prayer demands, on our part, a certain human continuity of existence and a certain conditioning of our being. Only a person accustomed to being attentive can agree not to flee into facile emotions or rational quibbling. He is present to that which is.

How can we describe this presence? The object of our prayer so drastically exceeds our powers. We could describe it by comparing it with the silence that we maintain in the room of a dying person. Unless we have lost our wits, we stay silent: the one about to die has secrets about which we have no inkling. Or again, it is like the confusion of a child, confronted for the first time in his life with the sorrow of grown-ups: those he loves the most in the whole world are in a universe that he cannot enter; he stops playing and snuggles up against his father and mother. To feel the hand of their child on their own is a momentary consolation for the sorrowing parents. Or again, the way we read the Passion might resemble the way we read, alone or with someone else, a letter recounting the last moments of a person dear to us. The distracted or superficial gaze, the heart that is dry or filled with self – these cannot maintain this presence.

To aid this delicate attention, it is good to re-read the various suggestions about prayer given during these ten days. They apply here more than ever before.

Practically speaking, it is impossible to exhaust the material in one day. One of the benefits of the thirty-day retreat is that it gives time to delay and return. At any rate, according to the time we have, we must find some helps. Thus, we can re-read one by one the four accounts of the evangelists. Or, using the method of the Way of the Cross or applying the categories given by St. Ignatius (consider what the Lord wants to endure in his humanity, how the divinity hides itself, how much he is enduring for my sins), we can remain first with one scene, then with another. We will soon give a few examples of this procedure. In any case, it is up to the individual, using these starting points. not to dwell upon his own reflections, but to let himself be penetrated by the person of Jesus.

We should not forget the usefulness of returning to the meditations we have already made. St. Ignatius, in connection with the Passion, insists strongly upon this point (*Ex.* 209).

THE DIFFICULTY: THE WALL

Often at this moment in the retreat, the retreatant runs into disconcerting difficulties – distractions, dryness, inability to concentrate, objections, rationalizations, temptations, the impression that he is wasting his time. On the other hand, he catches a glimpse of the riches hidden in this prayer. He does not want to abandon it, yet he wants something different. He is like a man who powerlessly and unfeelingly witnesses a scene of horror.

Perhaps, if you experience a similar uneasiness, you are on the way towards reaping the fruit of your prayer. Your feelings are neither those of exultation (which you would soon discover to be counterfeit) nor those of discouragement (for you are certain of being the object of an infinite love). The reason you are suffering is that you love so little and so poorly, that you stand before a wall which hides the mystery from you, a wall you cannot tear down. This suffering, as a matter of fact, places us in our real situation before Christ: receiving everything from him, yet powerless on our own to recognize the fullness of his gifts. We would have to receive from the Spirit the "strength to understand" (Eph. 3:18).

We find ourselves before the real difficulty of prayer, the difficulty of the wall of the invisible, beyond which we shall not cross unless and when God calls us. The other difficulties ought to be resolved. They come from the false or imperfect idea we have of prayer. Clarify it, and the difficulty disappears. What we are feeling here will not disappear, for it is prayer itself. It is a real purgatory, where man struggles with God in order to be grasped and transformed by him. The Passion makes us remain before this wall, until, one day, God makes the obstacle fall; and the joy of his presence will then console us for our many years of helpless waiting.

We experience this difficulty especially when confronted with the Passion, and this for two reasons. First, because of the object of prayer. This prayer does not allow us many references to ourselves, unlike the prayer of the preceding days. It is a more unselfish prayer, since the Lord occupies, or ought to occupy, the complete field of consciousness; yet is also a more austere prayer. The second reason is the unity of mood required by this prayer: it is so delicate that the least distracting breath spoils it. Faced with this prayer, we must agree to be truly poor.

This will seem overly simple to the person who limits himself to reasoning, but it will seem liberating to the person who has freely chosen to live. In fact, these mysteries are revealed only through being lived. They are part of that adventure of faith which we never finish living, as long as we are on this earth. Christ invested his whole life in going towards his Passion and in "freely entering" into it. We have no means for understanding the Passion of Christ other than to continue it in our own life and death. Everything will be explained when everything is consummated. Not before.

The simplest way is to let oneself be penetrated by a slow reading of the Passion narratives, whether in part or in their entirety. We explained this earlier. The following texts and thoughts might provide more food for prayer.

1. *The Prayer of the Suffering Just Man*

In his prayer, Jesus takes up the supplication of all men crushed by injustice and suffering. This supplication has been made in all places and in all ages. Some of its best expressions are found in those texts of the Old Testament which refer, in one way or another, to men's suffering. It is enough to cite just a few:

The blood of Abel: Gen. 4:8.
The story of Joseph: Gen. 37 to 50.
The long complaint of Job: Job.
The just and the unjust before the judgment of God: Wis. 2–5.
    Especially the humiliated Servant: Isaiah 52:13 to 53.
The persecutions against Jeremiah and his fidelity to God: Lamentations.
In the Epistle to the Hebrews (11 to 12:1–4), the list of the "cloud of witnesses" who endured the "test put before them" and whose leader is Jesus, he who "brings our faith to perfection".

Naturally, as done by the tradition of the Church and the liturgy, we can take up the psalms of the persecuted Just Man: Pss. 22(21), 38(37), 69(68), 75(74). Put into the mouth of Christ on the cross, such words take on an astounding resonance. Even the psalms' cries for vengeance, coming from the person who can no longer bear such violence and injustice, aptly express the cry of men of all times. Following the suggestion of St. Augustine in explaining these psalms: *Cum dicere coeperit, agnoscamus ibi nos esse.* When he begins to speak, realize that we are there.

2. *How Jesus Sees His Death (Jn. 12 and the Accounts of the Agony in the Synoptics)*

Jesus enters into his death with complete freedom and presence of mind (Newman, *The Moral Suffering of Jesus*). He shows this by the way he recognizes in the gesture of the woman who anoints his body an anticipation of his death. Moreover, he enters into his death like the awaited Messiah, the King of Israel: he accepts the triumphal entrance into Jerusalem.

But it is in a different way that he glorifies the Father and draws men to himself. Like the suffering Servant, it is through a death accepted out of love for the Father that he becomes fruitful and enters into life. It is along this road that he leads his followers. This hour makes him tremble; he but gives himself over to the Father, who manifests himself in the Passion.

The Synoptics dwell in a different way upon the dispositions of the Lord in the face of death. As if that were possible! Jesus is alone, left in agony. It is the hour of the prince of darkness. Jesus, after having prayed, plunges into it, dedicated to the will of the Father, while the flustered disciples fail to pray and, for the time being, remain strangers to the mystery. "Jesus is alone on the earth, not only in feeling and sharing his suffering, but even in merely knowing about it: heaven and he are the only ones with this knowledge" (Pascal).

In the presence of his Father, Jesus leaves the agony knowing what he is going to do. His Passion is an activity (Newman): "Before he was given up to death, a death he freely accepted", says the second Eucharistic Prayer.

Thus, in the presence of death, Jesus does not engage in self-pity or rationalization. He enters into it. He experiences the evil just as it is, in real suffering; but the justice he is seeking has a face, that of the Father. This justice consists in making that face of love manifest in all things; perfect like the heavenly Father is perfect, he does not utter a single word of hatred. That is why he begins his Passion standing up.

3. How Men Experienced the Passion: A Light on the Universal Drama

We can relive the Passion through its various actors – friends enemies, bystanders, the visible and invisible witnesses. Their reactions resemble those of men throughout the ages when faced with the suffering of the just and the innocent. Reading the Passion is a lesson for life.

First of all, there are the Powers. Jesus must appear before them all, one after another. The religious Powers: the chief priests and the Sanhedrin (Mt. 26:57-67). Jesus says what he has to say; then he remains silent. Condemned by the very persons who represent God on earth, he is not scandalized, nor does he speak a word of bitterness. Jesus is beautiful in his silence. But who understands his beauty? – Before the pagan political powers (Jn. 18:28 to 19:16), Jesus speaks the language of conscience and of truth, and then again becomes silent, secure in a realm that is closed to those who judge him. In him, the present world is already judged; and the walls that separate Jews and pagans collapse. All should recognize the need they have for one and the same Saviour. As he waits, Jesus goes before the powers of pleasure and money – the trial before Herod (Lk. 23:7-12). Between the two worlds present there, that of Jesus and that of Herod, there can be no meeting. The real splendour is on the side of Jesus. Yet the rich and silly playboy does not see it. The crowd, too, displays before Jesus its cowardice and inconstancy. It is a trial by the people (Mk. 15:6-15). Jesus becomes a plaything in the hands of the multitudes. Many others, before and after him, have known the same treatment. "It was our suffering that he bore" (Is. 53:4). Nothing was missing.

How do Jesus's friends react in the presence of the Passion? You will all be scandalized because of me, Jesus told them.

This scandal is expressed in the denial of Peter (Lk. 22:54–62). Peter is prepared for everything, even for giving his life – except for what really happens. He cannot understand Jesus's words: Put your sword in the sheath. The cup that my Father gave me to drink, . . . Could I not ask my Father . . .? Especially: Let these men go. It is as though Jesus wanted to go alone to his Passion. It is his "being sifted". All sorts of emotions clash together in Peter's soul. The first servant-girl and, even more so, the band of men can make him say anything at all: "I do not know that man." "You are the son of God," he had said (Mt. 16:16). He can no longer recognize him, covered as he is with humiliations. That will never happen to you (Mt. 16:22). It is only the gaze of Jesus as he passes that makes him remember and weep. It was true! A veil is torn open; a new world appears. We, too, have experienced such crises and such revelations.

Whoever wants to view the Passion of Jesus with Mary's eyes could look steadily at the evil of the world and "continue in his flesh what is lacking in the suffering of Christ" (Col. 1:24). Since the Annunciation, Mary, through the loss in the Temple and through Cana, has grown in the obscurity of faith. She is ready to recognize the Father's business, the hour. She stands upright at the foot of the cross. With Jesus, she goes to the very root of evil and is pure enough to overcome it in the suffering that it cost her. The new Eve at the side of the new Adam. Perfectly of one heart with him, she can, along with him, open her heart to universal love. This is your mother. This is your son. For her, Jesus is all mankind, those who find their salvation in Jesus. From now on, it is impossible to love him without loving along with him all those men whom he loves. In Mary begins the Church, the spouse of Christ, and the birth of all men into life and love.

4. *The Great Witness: The Father*

The Father is always with me. Jesus never stops repeating this throughout the entire Gospel of John. He repeats it more than ever before in his Passion. I can hear the mysterious conversation of the Father and the Son as the men unleash their torments against Jesus.

And, nevertheless, what does the Father do in the presence of the Son's suffering? He is silent, as God is silent before the evil of the world. He does not remove the evil; rather, he makes himself present there through his Son and overcomes evil through love.

When I look at Jesus in his Passion, God seems absent. For God is not in evil, in suffering, in death. God in the absence of God, Jesus speaks to his Father as if he were at a distance: Why have you abandoned me? Nevertheless, in this descent to the heart of evil – "descent into hell" – Jesus brings God to the world and manifests him. He lives the sign of sin – hatred, division, death – in love, without hatred. Bearing the curse, he delivers from it. He unveils in himself the victory of love, and in him the world can receive the Spirit once again.

Thus the Father's face is uncovered through the Passion, and the death of Christ becomes the revelation of the Three Persons. The Father reveals in Jesus the face of his mercy. The blood of Jesus becomes the witness of love (1 Jn. 5:6–8). His open side lets the riches of the Spirit flow out, the Church and the sacraments. The universe, insanely confused by its erring desires, rediscovers its path in the heart of each man and of all humanity, until, through the cross, each creature finds his way to God.

Before the cross, we make the Father hear our prayer for the the whole world (Liturgy of Good Friday). This prayer is sure to be heard: "Everything you ask in my name, I will do . . ." (Jn. 14:13–14).

5. *The Revelation of the Mystery (Eph. 3:14–21)*

Why does it happen like this? You may as well ask the Father, Son, and Spirit why they are Three. We stand before the mystery: love explains everything, but has no reason other than itself.

In order to enter into this mystery, we must "receive its strength". For the cross illuminates all reality in its "Width and Length, its Height and Depth". Through the cross we come to know "the love of Christ, which surpasses all knowledge". Through it we enter "fully into the perfect fullness of God". The cross "draws all things" to itself.

Its action continues in us, "along with all the saints". It is the fountain from which springs all brotherly love, all action, all suffering within the Church. The Christian, illuminated by the cross, allows love to operate within him and, even if rejected by men, along with Peter who is no longer scandalized, he "entrusts his soul to his faithful creator" (1 Peter 4:12–19). The language of the cross becomes a wisdom for life (1 Cor. 1:17 to 2).

Every effort at discernment leads to the recognition of the glorious cross. Thus we can understand why it is good to return unceasingly to the meditation of the Passion. "I will frequently recall the sufferings, the fatigue, and the sorrows which Christ our Lord bore from the moment of his birth up to the mystery of the Passion, in which I am presently engaged" (Ex. 206).

X. The New Man: The Risen Christ

The Purpose of the Day: A Transition

Why the victorious cross? Not because of itself, but because of him who took it up. There Jesus brings victory over hatred, the source of death. He lives through all things, even death, in love. In living love to the very end, Jesus unites himself with the Father in the midst of the evil he is immersed in. He is the first among men to pass from death to life, because he has loved. Love alone, when it is called God-made-man, triumphs over all. Thus, glory transfigures his humanity. After him, we are transformed along with him: having passed from death to life because we have loved. The new life is a life in love and justice. It is imperishable.

Living in the risen Christ, I can resume my life and my place in the world without becoming bogged down in it, leading the world not to ruin but rather to the transfiguration it awaits. I have discovered in the risen Jesus the sources of genuine freedom, the kind that consists in loving God in all things. The risen Christ becomes the perfect man, and in him all things human are led to God.

In the risen Christ, the spiritual experience finds the goal of its movement. Easter completes the movement out of self that was begun at the start of the *Exercises*. Or rather, the end joins up with the beginning by revealing to us what it includes. Then Christ appeared to us as the one who had lived in his humanity the return of all things to God in genuine freedom. We discover ourselves in him, making all things return to God with him and through his cross. The movement of the Spirit continues from him to us. Through today's Church, Christ makes those who belong to him enter into glory.

Joy, unity, apostolic spirit, brotherly love, a sense of the Church – these are the fruits of this day. Today should teach us

a bit more about that new way of living which consists in finding
God in all things and in doing all things out of love.

PRAYER BEFORE THE RISEN CHRIST

It confronts us with the danger at the end of every retreat:
various regrets, reasons for leaving before the end, fatigue, fear
of the life facing us again, uneasiness about the coming demands
upon our fidelity. Whoever thinks that the retreat has completely transformed him soon discovers evidence to the contrary
in the way he lives out this final day. It is a wholesome experience, one which removes his last illusions.

Seriously, let's not leave the retreat like schoolchildren leaving for their vacation. The transition to everyday life should
take place in faith and in the most natural way possible. The
urge to live out this realism is the sign of a transition to an adult
faith. God is no longer to be sought in the imagination, in
pictures, or in feelings, but in a more intense presence to our
real-life situation. We have spoken about the transition from
the intellectual, psychological, and moral levels to the level of
faith and the Spirit. We do not have to wait until the end of
the retreat in order to put it into practice. This last day gives
us the opportunity we are looking for. Here we can live that
dedication of self which, under its most varied forms, is our
election.

The quality of today's prayer is continuous with that of the
two preceding days. It still demands a great interior silence in
the midst of all the concerns that have already begun to assail
us. Its joy is not the exuberance of a cheerful temperament;
rather, it roots itself in a deeply felt presence of the Holy Spirit
in our hearts.

The joy we ask for here is a fruit of the Holy Spirit. One of the
greatest graces a person can obtain in this world is to discover
that, in his desire for Christ alone, he can find God in all
circumstances and can live contentedly anywhere. Rejoice
without ceasing (Phil. 4:4). The entire passage of Phil. 4:4–9
should be meditated upon from this perspective.

Even if there is not enough time to follow up with the

"contemplation to obtain the love of God", this meditation nevertheless is especially fitting for this day. It is the prayer of our entire life: the work of God contemplated here below in the risen Christ, so that we might offer ourselves more fully to his movement of life. The scenes of the Resurrection and Ascension lead us to Pentecost, where the power of the Spirit sends us to preach the Gospel to all creatures. These scenes make up the everyday prayer of the Church.

THE RETURN TO THE BEGINNING

On the first day, we recalled the creation of man in the image of God. It is only in the risen Christ that we understand the meaning of this expression, not to make us dwell in contemplation upon it, but that we might be transformed day after day into that image, through the action of the Lord who is Spirit (2 Cor. 3:18).

1. *The New Man*

Man begins with the risen Jesus. He emerges in Jesus from the hands of the Creator. Adam again meets the Christ who has come to hell to take him away. The Paradise which we have situated at the beginning is actually in the future. We must create paradise along with Christ. That is how Peter makes us see these things on the morning of Pentecost (Acts 2): Jesus fulfils the hope announced to the men of old; he is the consummation, he is immortality. A world begins with him. His glorified flesh becomes the centre of every life in the Spirit.

The Resurrection is the summit that clarifies everything – history and Scripture. Beginning with it, we are able to read both of these. Illuminated by the grace of Easter, we see Christ everywhere. "He opened their minds so they could understand Scripture" (Lk. 24:45). The attitude of the just and poor man, which he maintained up to the cross and which finds its fulfilment in the Resurrection, continues in us within the Church. His resurrected life constitutes a life of justice in us.

It is also a new presence, inaccessible to the eyes of the flesh. The world will not see me, yet you will see me. An essential saying that reveals the secret of the new life – the community of life in the Spirit. We are present to him because we are living according to his commandment of love. A new relationship according to the heart and freedom. This presence is given to us in the midst of this world that is continuing. As St. John vividly portrays it, this "glory" begins in the intimate depths of the cross and produces the Transfiguration in those whom it draws into a kind of Exodus.

2. *The Church*

It is born with the risen Christ as the place of love founded on faith in Jesus. In the Church, there takes place the encounter between man's aspiration towards love and the Creator's response to this aspiration, an encounter of two dynamisms, ascending and descending, which takes place in Christ, who is both man and God.

The risen Christ, living in the Church and sought by us in the Eucharist, preserves us simultaneously from an anxious kind of fidelity which prevents growth and from a frantic kind of adaptation which is nothing but the fear of failure. The Church is not a society of the untainted, established in perfection and forcing all men to submit to its rule. It is that transitional place where, through sinful men, we discover the face of Christ: "Whatever you do to the least of these little ones . . . Whoever hears you hears me . . ." The lowliest person, just as much as someone in authority, becomes Christ for us. In faith, the contradictions begin to collapse. In each of us, the Church is on the march, not towards some golden age but towards the Revelation of a mystery that we already possess. The Church is at the heart of the world and in the heart of each of us.

In the Church, I see the diversity of particular vocations. These gain their value from their reference to the love that gave them birth. I rediscover myself in all of them, as if they were my own vocations, though I myself am in the vocation that God gives me. It is not important whether it is you or I who have received this gift. Whether it is you or I, it is Christ who lives it out.

Towards those men who are hostile to the Church or who remain outside it, the Christian living the mystery of the Church has neither a contemptuous nor a propagandist attitude. He has the sense of mission, but in the style of Christ, sent by the Father into the world. Wherever he is, in accordance with his own vocation, he is a Presence, so that through him the Fullness might be realized. Thus, in whatever particular place he lives his mortal life, he lives a total and universal love, in the spirit of the First Epistle of John.

In order to be lived, this mystery of the incarnate Word demands a perpetual rupture, that of the transition from the flesh to the spirit. "You are blessed, Simon Peter, for it is not flesh and blood that have revealed this to you but my Father." This revelation of the Father to an open heart makes us discover, in the Church as in the incarnate Word, the presence of God in the humiliation of the flesh, the scandal of the continuing Incarnation. It is in accepting this scandal that the spiritual life becomes Christian.

At the heart of this mystery, Mary is present. In the Cenacle, awaiting the Spirit along with the apostles, she is the reconciled humanity. Her presence at the heart of the Church makes us discover and live out her mystery.

3. *God in All Things: Freedom*

In the grace of Easter, Jesus begins to live in each of his disciples the ministery of Reconciliation through his universal priesthood. Through him, all things move towards the Father within a creation that shapes and renews itself. In this movement, the Eucharist celebrated in the community of the disciples holds a central place.

We share the realities we live with all other men, but in a new manner of existing and acting – not domination but love. In his apparitions, Christ shows himself as simple and brotherly. This is how the whole human situation can be lived in him. The most simple persons, to whom the risen Jesus reveals himself, experience God in the present.

Again in him, we experience a lived kind of freedom. No longer a dry, pretentious, or vindictive kind of freedom – which betrays the insufficiencies and fears of a person who is searching for himself; rather, a freedom which is the acquiescence of each person in the present reality, in the certitude that all things work together for the good of those who love.

The constraints and the servitudes of this present existence take on a new meaning for him. They are no longer undergone in fear and resignation. They are the burdens of love, borne in company with him who went to the very depths of our servitudes and who was the first to free us from the radical servitude, that of sin. His freedom – and our freedom in him – permits us to love even in the midst of the constraints that weigh upon man. With him, in the concrete situation we find ourselves in, we work for the liberation of all men, in the spirit that was his own.

As the end of the *Exercises* unfolds, the individual is brought back to his occupations – to the beginning – renewed a bit more in the Spirit and in fraternal love. Many questions that were raised at the beginning remain unanswered. It is enough if we have learned to face them in a new way. Earlier I asked: Should I continue this or that? Faced now with the risen Christ, how should I answer? I decide to set out on the road again. Let's not look for anything more. Let's live. Each day has enough troubles of its own. Tomorrow will bring its answer.

HELPS FOR TODAY'S PRAYER

There are many appropriate readings for the time of Easter. We can at least keep the following: the discourse after the Last Supper, the First Epistle of St. John, and the texts already cited in the preceding reflections. From among the many rich scenes in the Gospel, we could choose the following:

1. *How the Risen Jesus Is Present to His Mother*

St. Ignatius invites us to contemplate Christ's apparition to

Mary. To justify this, he merely says: "Scripture presupposes that we have good sense." It is, in fact, a spiritual understanding that we need to grasp what kind of new world Jesus and Mary have entered (*Ex.* 299).

They have become one in heart: at the foot of the cross, Mary united herself to the intention of her Son. It is this presence in the Spirit that constitutes their unity. It is this presence that the Resurrection has brought about: Christ is present to those who are united with him in their heart. The body is no longer opaque; it has become the expression and the transparency of the spirit.

A new life begins, a new mode of being, this spiritual presence that death cannot interrupt. The world cannot grasp this presence: "The world will no longer see me. You, however, will see me, because I live and you shall live" (Jn. 14:19).

Let us say that in Mary a new stage of creation has been inaugurated. The winter has passed, the rains have ended (Song of Songs 2:8–14): a presence through the Spirit, through freedom and love. Especially: through the glorious humanity of Jesus, Mary enters into the depths of the mystery of God. She comes to know him, always beyond everything, like a sea without shores. Life begins for her in the transformation of love, a transformation to which mankind has been committed.

What can we say about this new stage? Only faith and spiritual understanding can penetrate into it.

It is along the lines of this presence of Christ to his mother that we should explain the meeting of Jesus and Magdalene (Jn. 20: 11–18). She has entered into a presence of love that is maintained only to the extent that the person receiving it consents to ceaselessly go beyond the knowledge already accorded him. "O you who are beyond everything!" (St. Gregory Nazianzen).

2. *How Jesus Manifests Himself to the Disciples of Emmaus (Lk. 24:13–35)*

Jesus initiates them progressively to this new presence, making himself known to them by the effects of his action: presence in joy, presence in the Spirit, presence in brotherly love. In him, the active and dynamic presence of the Spirit is communicated to us.

They are sad as they meet Jesus; and, starting with the reasons behind their sadness, he leads them to joy. This is the first effect of the Resurrection: he takes man in his entirety; and beginning with man's present state, he draws out what man most profoundly is. The cross is still present; but, thanks to the understanding of Scriptures he gives them, the cross shines with the glory of the Spirit. The Resurrection gives unmixed joy. Yet, even though he is already present, they do not know that it is he. He has merely restored hope, awakened joy, roused desire: "Stay with us."

At their request, he stays with them. Yet precisely at the moment that they recognize him in the breaking of the bread, he has already disappeared from them. In fact, "the breaking of the bread", or the revelation of his glorious body, causes another transition in them, the transition from an external kind of presence to the true presence, that of the Spirit, where persons become interior to one another in love. Definitely, it is good that he goes, that he disappears from the eyes of the flesh in order to make himself present in the heart that lives through him by faith. "If anyone loves me, he will keep my commandment; and my Father will love him, and we will come to him and make our dwelling place with him." The world is unconscious of this presence. Just as before, it continues to scurry about its business. In the famous painting of Rembrandt, the servant girl continues to wash the dishes. The change produced by the Lord's Resurrection does not take place on the level of appearances. For the man who looks with his eyes of flesh, there is nothing but the empty tomb.

This intimate presence becomes a fraternal presence, the

presence of those who, each on his own, have come to know experientially that Jesus is risen. Each one at first thinks that he is alone and wants to tell the others the great news: the two disciples return to Jerusalem, to find their brothers again. They discover that those whom they wanted to inform about the wonder know about it too: it is really true! He has shown himself to you? To us too! A community is formed – Christ known in the Church.

The apostles begin to take on the shape of the glorious Christ. Once we have recognized him, we never finish discovering him – in events, in the Eucharist, in brotherly living, in Scripture, and in prayer (Acts 2:42). He is never discovered completely, so long as he has not yet appeared totally in all things. As long as we are in our mortal condition, we are on our way towards him who is, however, already present (2 Cor. 4:7–5:10).

3. *How Jesus Is Present in the Brotherly Community (Jn. 21)*

This manifestation is an "epiphany" of the Lord. But it no longer takes place in the thunder and lightning of Sinai. The Christ of glory is present in everyday life and in the most humble meeting of brothers. Jesus is there in his usual way, simultaneously present and drawing us beyond the present.

He is present in the work of men, even when they are unconscious of this. Besides, they have no time for thinking about him; their work and the irritation at having caught nothing absorbs them too much. Nevertheless, what unites them in this very ordinary work is his word: "I will go before you into Galilee"; thus, it is the love that he has put into their hearts.

At daybreak, each one recognizes Jesus in his own manner. John first, for he discovers the reality beneath the signs. He hears the voice, sees the gestures, notices the effects of the casting of the net. As at the empty tomb, he sees and he believes (Jn. 20:8). There are two distinct operations here. Once he has made his discovery, John enjoys it in silence and continues his work. Peter, more demonstrative, cannot contain himself: he swims in to meet the Lord. Luckily the others do not imitate him; otherwise the fish would have got away. There are various kinds of charismata. There are various ways of discovering the Lord in the unity of the same love.

The time of discourses is past. The time for silent love has come: Jesus prepares the meal for his friends. No action-project, just a few minutes of intimacy. If one day they witness with their lives that they have seen and touched, it is in the memory of the moments lived now. No one dared to ask, for they all knew it was the Lord. We must never balk before such moments, apparently wasted, for they are the proof that love exists.

Peter testifies to his brotherly love. That is the sense of the triple question, "Do you love me?" Peter shows by his answer that he now recognizes the source of love. He no longer says, "Whatever the others might do, I will follow you"; but rather, "You know." In the same way that the Father communicated to him faith in the Son, the faith of which Peter is the foundation (Mt. 16:13–20), he now communicates to him the love of which Peter is the guarantor among men: "Feed my sheep." This is the function of Peter within the Church: he holds the primacy in faith and love; it is he who "presides over love" (St. Catherine of Sienna). All government in the Church is a function of love (Lk. 22:24–7). The superior is the sign of unity, "the one who creates the unity of all his men" (Nadal). Obedience is not a material or uneasy fidelity; it is a mutual help for remaining in that unity without which Christ is not present.

Whatever will be the destiny of the individuals in the community, the important thing is not the work itself but the way in which it is done. More than the others, Peter needs to hear the words: "When you were young, you went wherever you wanted to", you gave me advice and led the way. There is coming a time in life when we will understand that, though we think we are giving ourselves, we are in fact being taken, and that our greatest activity consists in letting ourselves be led "where we do not want to go". This is the turning point of existence. Then we will begin to glorify the Lord; we will begin to die so that we might enter into life. After that point, what does the destiny of each individual matter? Peter dies in this way, John in that. What does it matter? You, follow me. God glorifies himself in the variety of gifts and destinies. The important thing is not to look alike in our external works but, in our various works, to grow in love and mutual respect.

When we have gone this deep, is there any point in distinguishing the human from the divine, action from contemplation? The profound unity of the person takes place in that constant loss of self that opens a person up to God and makes God known in the experience of his Spirit. Our differences are washed away in the wake of that love that "eclipses the sun and the other stars" (Dante).

4. *How Jesus Remains Present in the Church: The Ascension*
   (Acts 1:1–11)

The Holy Spirit began his work in the womb of Mary through the Annunciation; he continues it in the Church through the Ascension. In both cases, he forms the body of Christ, first of all in his state of humiliated servant, then in the glory of the Father. These two beginnings are marked by the presence and consent of Mary: at Nazareth and in the Cenacle. In her, the creature consents to the work of the Creator.

The Lord Jesus remains present now in the Church, no longer in his earthly presence, not yet in his glorious presence, but rather "snatched" from the eyes so that he might be awaited and prepared for. Through his Spirit, he remains present in the sacrament and through the mission. The Eucharist opens up to the mission so that his body might extend to the entire universe and so that the universe might become the Eucharist. Then he will come again in glory.

The mission he leaves his followers is not to found or restore a Kingdom, but rather to reveal the love of the Father, who through Christ gives the Spirit so that all mankind might participate in the life of God. Having received this mission, the disciples should neither continue to gape at the sky nor to get wrapped up in the affairs of the earth, but rather, throughout the history of the world, to show men that they are in the Spirit: "Proclaim the Good News to all creation" (Mk. 16:15). "You have seen merely the beginning of the wonders. You shall see the heavens open and the angels of God ascending and descending upon the Son of Man" (Jn. 1:50–1).

BRINGING THE EXPERIENCE TO A CLOSE

EVALUATION AND FINAL SHARING

Has the time come to make an evaluation? Maybe in six months. . . . Judge the tree by its fruits. For the moment, we are lucky if the tree has begun to blossom. Actually, we are like the disciples of Emmaus who thought that everything was over, though it was just beginning for them. In bringing the experience to a close, the danger is to linger with the memories of what we have gone through. Let us not stop advancing "from faith to faith" (Rm. 1:17).

If it is not good to linger too long on the results, it still might be good to share the experience we have had with those who have accompanied us: a brotherly sharing that makes us accept one another in the Spirit. We could go around the circle, each one responding, for example, to the following question: *what difference has the experience of these ten days made in my way of viewing human life, spiritual life, fraternal life?*

A simple exchange of the lights we have received.

KEEPING THE EXPERIENCE ALIVE

It is normal that this question arise, even if it contains some unhealthy worries. At least, in establishing a life-project, we should be concerned more about spiritual structures that maintain a way of life than about rules and practices that we often cannot keep.

Among such structures, we can insist upon the following:

1. *Prayer*

A certain kind of prayer develops out of the *Exercises*. It has been called *methodical* – not in the sense that it imposes limits, but rather in the sense that it proposes starting points or experiments that teach the individual how to ready himself for the grace of God. We should say that the method of the *Exercises* tries to maintain a certain orientation of the heart, so that our deepest desires can come clearly to the surface and be fulfilled.

This purification, moreover, takes place especially in the experience of love and in the search for those spiritual gifts which make us deeply feel and taste reality. That is why prayer finds its ordinary food in the mysteries of the life of Christ and in Scripture, read and meditated in rhythm with the Liturgy.

Finally, this prayer, more affective than intellectual, could be called "practical". First of all, in the sense that it looks for a certain commitment of the person, just as the *Exercises* look for an election. However, it does not seek so much to shed light upon the things we have to do, the decisions we have to make, the projects we have to accomplish; all this is dependent upon the resources of our practical intelligence. Rather, it helps to spread upon that whole undertaking the "unction" of the Spirit. It is not a pause or an interruption in our activity; rather it communicates to our activity simultaneously gentleness and strength, patience and enthusiasm, power and resiliency, and especially peace and confidence.

We could add that, far from opposing action, this prayer presupposes it and supports it. It finds in action the criterion of its genuineness, just as it preserves action from illusions by harmonizing it with the will of God.

2. *The Repetitions*

There are retreats. In a little while, we shall say something about the renewal of this experience.

Days of recollection have come into wide use. We can still ask ourselves if they achieve what they set out to do. Perhaps, like retreats, they become too quickly an established institution that answers no real need. It is up to the individual, in this whole matter, to discover his own rhythm and his own way, whatever we choose to call it. The important thing is that the spirit live.

3. *Keeping Alive on the Intellectual Level: Continuing to Learn*

It is useless to repeat here the ideas developed in *Le Prêtre à la recherche de lui-même* (Le Chalet, 1969). At the end of these ten days, it suffices to insist on three points. First, the necessity of bringing one's religious learning up to the level of one's human learning. A faith that remains on the infantile level cannot stand up long in the face of scientific developments and human progress. Otherwise it becomes an isolated domain without any ties with life. Then again, in this effort to keep abreast intellectually, no one should go beyond his depth. Especially in the religious realm, nothing is more unpleasant than people whose words, totally without foundation in experience, merely repeat the words of others or of books. There is more genuineness in those simple persons who stay close to life. Finally, let us add (and this point of view has inspired more than one remark during these ten days) how dangerous it is not to take into account the human development and experience of the person undertaking this adventure. Such a spiritual life clearly risks being riddled with illusions.

A LIFE OF DISCERNMENT: THE EXAMEN

The examen is, in fact, the great means (according to Ignatius, more important than prayer) for maintaining the experience had during the *Exercises*. Of course, it could be viewed on a very ordinary level as a means of correcting one's faults and of developing good habits. From this point of view, the examen does serve some useful purpose, but it does not go beyond the efforts of a man who wants to make himself acceptable in his social milieu or to succeed in an enterprise.

The *Exercises* make us see the examen in a different light, as an attempt to re-establish the whole person in the direction of the election, in order to give still more room to the action of the Spirit after the person's inevitable failures. Re-situated thus within the perspectives of the purification of heart, which aims at a greater docility to the Holy Spirit in the midst of action, the examen becomes part of the great spiritual tradition that extends from St. Paul, through the Eastern tradition and St. Francis Xavier, all the way to St. Therese of the Child Jesus.

St. Paul (2 Cor. 12:7–9) asks God to be delivered from the thorn that had been lodged in his flesh. God answers him: "My grace is enough for you; my strength operates in the midst of weakness." It is not important to explain the thorn in the flesh. What counts is to turn an obstacle into a means for making the power of God shine forth in me: the strength of his arm operates in the humble ones (*Magnificat*).

In the same sense, but with more precision, the Eastern tradition counsels a daily manifestation, or filtering, of thoughts in the frequent remembrance of the Lord Jesus. Descending to the depths of our consciousness, among all the images that are found there and which we can discover, we let the image of the Lord Jesus, who is living in our hearts, come more and more to the fore.

St. Francis Xavier, in the great letter he wrote from Japan on "the understanding of hope in God", counsels those who dream of doing great things to prepare themselves by working to maintain confidence in God in the midst of the little things. These little things are not the occasions for assuring ourselves of our own merits; rather, they are the means of experiencing the weakness of our flesh and the ever-greater need we have to entrust ourselves to God.

In the same tradition, we could cite Lallemant, Surin, de Coussade, etc.

St. Therese of the Child Jesus says the same thing in her own words: "The more a person is feeble and miserable, the more fit he is for the operations of that consuming and transforming love. . . ." "The real difficulty is to consent to remain always poor and without strength."

Each one, in his own way, expresses an attitude that is fundamentally the same for all: to turn everything into an occasion for entrusting oneself to God, certain that, if an obstacle is lived through in Christ, even it becomes a means. Here we rediscover that attitude of an exchange of love which we mentioned in connection with penitence, an attitude whose expression is found in the sacrament. From this point of view, the examen daily prepares us better for confession.

The most lively expression of this attitude belongs perhaps to St. Alphonsus Rodriguez. It sums up in a simple formula all the elements described above: "Whenever I experience bitterness", he writes, "I place this bitterness between God and myself, until he changes it into sweetness." The bitterness is a fact. And if I try simply to chase away this bitterness (or any other emotion I condemn), I risk merely increasing my difficulty. I become like the person who is so afraid of falling that he falls. Many falls stem from antecedent flights. Still, I cannot simply capitulate to what I feel in me, to this interior division that St. Paul mentions in Romans 7. Thus, I turn this acknowledged obstacle into a means: I show the Lord this state I am in, so that he might change it. And I continue to begin again, until the very end. This means putting the Lord in the very heart of the disorder I find myself in. Here we are fully situated in the realm of freedom and grace. I make use of the fear of freedom I find in myself, in order to give myself over more entirely to grace; and, transformed by grace and in increased freedom, I give myself even more.

As we are presenting it here, the examen makes us capable of finding God in all things and of discerning his work in us. More than a mere recognition of the presence of God, the examen becomes a means for co-operating with God's action upon me and upon the world. For various reasons I can be unable to find the time for a period of prayer. But I am never dispensed from making the examen, no more than I am dispensed from living.

THE CONTEMPLATION TO OBTAIN LOVE (*Ex.* 230–7)

The contemplation suggested here at the end is more than just another exercise; it describes a way of living in the midst of the world and a way of praying in all circumstances. It can be made during the retreat, but it is intended especially for those leaving the retreat who want to keep its spirit.

Everything here is centred upon love, because love is the fundamental and final reality: God is love, and he manifests himself in works of love – creation, the gift of his Son and of the Spirit, the divinization of man. Living in the world, and without closing my eyes, I can therefore ask to be able to recognize God's action everywhere, so that I can love and serve him in everything. The liberation begun in the *Exercises*, maintained by the examen (as I have just presented it), is what we can do for our part to make this prayer possible. Seeking to abandon ourselves, we can open ourselves to love.

This love does not come from us. We cannot whip ourselves up into loving; we ask to receive it. For it is the Spirit poured out into our hearts. There are two objective criteria for this love (or of its presence in us), those which St. John presents in his epistle: on the one hand, it is deed; on the other, it is sharing. We do not love in words but "in deed and in truth" (1 John 3:18). Not just any deed (It could be the deed of the Pharisee who makes himself seen and thus has received his reward); rather, the deed that establishes equality and communion between persons who love one another. The cross is the manifestation of this love, to the degree that it leads to the Trinity and opens up the well-springs of life. The disciple of Jesus, who has received his Spirit, lives in his daily life this unending transition from deed to sharing; and, in living it, he learns what God is.

In order to let himself be caught up by this love, he prays, using a few points of departure. But each time, his prayer, like Jesus's, leads to self-giving: "Take and receive, Lord." The substance of this gift is myself and all that makes me up: especially my freedom, along with everything else I have and live. This gift leaves out nothing; for everything is received from God in an act of sharing, so that it might be returned in love. Man becomes God's co-worker, like the Son who receives everything from the Father and returns it to him in the communication of the Spirit. It is an unending movement through which the will of God is accomplished. So that this movement might carry me even further along, I ask just one thing: Love and Grace.

This manner of praying is called "contemplation", yet a contemplation which, taken up into the movement of self-abandonment generated by the *Exercises*, tends to suppress the distance that separates ideal and activity, heart and deed, self and others.

It is towards this kind of contemplation (which is, for that matter, a way of acting) that the formation given by the *Exercises* tends. He had become a "contemplative in action", Nadal writes of St. Ignatius; that is, he found God no less in action, in work, in study, in relationships, than he did in prayer. Everything had become God for him. That is why, wherever he was, he was at ease – something that showed in the way his face beamed and in the peace that he radiated. To him, for whom God had become all, each thing had become important. There lies the secret of the intense presence which a person living in this spirit can have in everything he does. He does not need to protect the presence of God by efforts extrinsic to whatever it is he is doing. He lives God in all things.

In order to maintain this way of living, St. Ignatius suggests four points. Although they are interconnected in the unity of the dynamics of love, it is not necessary to meditate on them together. In each point, all the others are contained. It suffices to grasp their intent and then to take one or the other, according to the need we experience.

The first point is a meditation of recollection. It condenses in itself all the other points, in somewhat the same way that the Foundation contains in germ the rest of the *Exercises*. All the good things of the universe and of the whole history of man can enter into this prayer. The essential thing is to "ponder with a lot of love" what has happened, in order to let myself be grasped by the love of "the divine plan". We can never really understand things apart from the love that made them exist.

The second point takes up the movement of things, in order to grasp more deeply their meaning. The vast evolution of the universe, from the vegetative to the intelligent, moves through its successive stages towards a more and more intimate presence of God to his creature. The entire universe is tending towards the transfiguration: at the end, "he made me his people, having created me" in his image and likeness.

God is not exterior to the gifts he gives me; he is working within his gifts, to lead his creature to its goal. That is the purpose of the third point: it is addressed to our heart, to invite us to consider God's efforts for man within the universe in Jesus Christ.

Finally, the fourth point situates me at the heart of the God-head, from which I see all things proceeding like the rays of the sun or like water flowing from its source. The never-ending movement of descent and return. God is the ocean that has no shores. No formula can grasp him. Everything comes from him, yet he is beyond everything. In him we find unity, yet we can never reach the end. Eternal life is precisely this welling forth.

After each point, the "Suscipe" becomes the habitual prayer. In the Spirit whom the Father communicates to me, with the Son at the heart of the Trinity, I "make restitution" to God for all the things he has given me. Not, however, a restitution that is merely the return of unimproved talents; for creation has drawn interest in the hands of man, so that all things might enter into the one, sole Love. The world is not a closed system.

HELPS FOR THIS CONTEMPLATION

All of Scripture nourishes this contemplation, when it is read in the spirit of respect and thanksgiving that befits it. The entire life of man, too, in its details and its main lines, becomes an occasion for this prayer. Just a few remarks will suffice. Each individual must find his own way to be a "contemplative in action".

The prayer of the Psalms is valuable, especially if we are able to hold on to this or that verse which, repeated over a period of time, helps to maintain our attention on the reality. We can mention the Psalms of praise, as well as those that recount the gracious deeds of God in the history of Israel. At this time, why not return to Psalm 139(138), which we meditated on at the start? At the end of this experience, it takes on a new meaning and can help measure the road we have travelled.

Moreover, recalling again the itinerary followed during the retreat can serve as a unifying thread for prayer. Through a quick summary it can help us glimpse the effect of the whole. This is also an excellent way of making the examination of conscience such as we have presented it: making ourselves present again to the action of God, this very day, in order to co-operate more fully with it.

Above all, the earnest meditation of the First Letter of John is perhaps the best scriptural transposition of the contemplation for love. There God makes himself known through the effects of his action: light (1 to 2) and love (3 to 4). In us, the participation in his gifts follows the same rhythm; it moves from the knowledge and admission of sin to our transformation in God, propelled by fidelity to the commandment of love. This action is the work of God. Clearly, we recognize God in the love we have for one another. The active presence of God in our faith, which is our "victory over the world" (5).

More than ever before, this prayer is centred upon the Eucharist, *the* act of thanksgiving, in which are summarized all the marvels of God and which gives meaning to the daily evolution of our lives. More than one of the eucharistic texts can be helpful for this prayer.

We are no longer in the retreat. Nevertheless the action of the Spirit continues its work in us. Prayer maintains us in his presence.

THE RENEWAL OF THIS
EXPERIENCE

No retreat, if it is an experience of the life of the Spirit, can resemble the preceding one. For, between the two, life has continued and has changed us. That is why we must never try to rediscover the past experience. We can only retain the memory of it, so that we might move further on.

The itinerary and method we have followed have established structures in us that permit both fidelity and inventiveness. We know where to begin and how to conduct ourselves, without locking ourselves up within a rigid formula. This antecedent formation permits us to begin the new retreat in the freedom of the Spirit.

How should we do it? When should we renew this experience? It is as difficult to answer these questions as it is to answer those others: when should I receive the sacraments, and how should I prepare myself for them? Evidently there are a few simple rules that help us in undertaking things we have not yet experienced. Yet, the more the experience grows, the more the individual is led to follow his own path. If your procedure stems from love, there is no danger of succumbing to illusions or of falling into isolation.

At the end of this experience, especially if it has been renewed in retreats of ten or thirty days, we are tempted to insist more upon freedom than upon exactitude. Many people, because they have never dared to fly with their own wings, have never exercised the radiance and fruitfulness in the Church that one would expect from the gifts they received. They have remained faithful servants at a time when they were called to friendship and creativity.

The only thing left to do is to experience it. After several years in which you have remained faithful to the education given by the *Exercises*, go spend eight days alone in a monastery or some other quiet place. Do not take much – the Bible should be enough – and just live in the presence of God. Nadal, in his commentary on the Constitutions of St. Ignatius, presents the ideal of prayer for the so-called "formed" Jesuit (Is he ever really formed?) saying, *"sinant suo spiritu duci"*: "nothing should be imposed on them", he says; "they should be allowed to be led by the spirit that is in them". Prematurely given, this rule could lead to disasters. The inconstancy of some persons to whom we might give this rule would prevent them from successfully living out this freedom. Nevertheless, this rule is liberating and necessary for those whose heart is full of the desire to serve God with their entire self. Certainly they still need counselling. Yet, the more our life advances, the more difficult it becomes to find the counselling we need to go fearlessly in the direction of that increasingly exigent freedom. Still, persons have a sense for other persons. It is enough to have met somewhere along the way that spiritual Father (It does not matter whether he is a priest, a friend, a director, a brother; here these labels no longer have their usual meaning) and to see him again from time to time, to continue the conversation of a year ago, as though it was just yesterday that we parted company. Through him, we know that the light does exist and that we are securely travelling the same road with him – and with many others whom we have not yet met.